Decisionmaker

David Evans

CAMBRIDGE
UNIVERSITY PRESS

PUBLISHED BY THE PRESS SYNDICATE OF THE UNIVERSITY OF CAMBRIDGE
The Pitt Building, Trumpington Street, Cambridge, United Kingdom

CAMBRIDGE UNIVERSITY PRESS
The Edinburgh Building, Cambridge CB2 2RU, UK
40 West 20th Street, New York, NY 10011–4211, USA
477 Williamstown Road, Port Melbourne, VIC 3207, Australia
Ruiz de Alarcón 13, 28014 Madrid, Spain
Dock House, The Waterfront, Cape Town 8001, South Africa

http://www.cambridge.org

First published 1997
Fourth printing 2003

Printed in the United Kingdom at the University Press, Cambridge

ISBN 0 521 44805 0

Contents

Thanks and acknowledgments

The author would like to thank Will Capel, Sarah Almy and Jayshree Ramsurun at Cambridge University Press for their advice and support on the project. Thanks also to Stephen Bryant, Patrick Collins and Richard Moberly for their help with some technical details.

The author and publishers would like to thank the following individuals and institutions for their help in piloting and commenting on the material and for the invaluable feedback which they provided:

David Cordell, Eurocentre, Alexandria; Leigh Fergus, Formation and Communication, Paris; Alison Haill, Oxford Academy, Oxford, England; Sarah Jones-Macziola, International House, Freiburg, Germany; Peter Lake, International House, Toulouse, France; Rod Revell, Hong Kong Polytechnic; Will Sykes, The Bell School of Languages, Cambridge, England; Patricia Trainor, University of Málaga, Spain; Juliana Zimmerman, Insearch Language Centre, Sydney, Australia.

The author and publishers are grateful to the following photographic sources and copyright holders for permission to reproduce material in the text:

p22 Telegraph Colour Library; p23 © Tony Stone Images; p35 © Mark Henley/Impact; p43, 45 and 86 © Image Bank; p44 Roger Howard/Ace; p52 © Pictor International; p77 © *The Economist*, London (16.06.90); p86 Mauritius/Ace.

Illustrations on pp5, 12, 18, 30, 34, 53, 83 and 95 by Tony Morris. All other illustrations by Oxford Illustrators.

Book designed by MetaDesign London and produced by Oxprint Design.

How to use *Decisionmaker*

Decisionmaker is a teacher's resource book for use with students of Business English at intermediate levels and above. The core of the book is formed by a number of problems, each one designed to provide a natural springboard for discussion. Most of them deal with familiar moral, social and personal problems set in realistic business contexts, so making them accessible to Business English learners with or without experience of the world of work.

Decisionmaker explores many varied aspects of business around the world, from video piracy in Moscow to computer software development in Bangalore. It can be integrated into a traditional Business English course to provide practice in reading, fluency and communication skills. Equally, individual chapters can form the basis of a 'Business Option' on a General English course.

The book is intended to be as flexible as possible, so each unit offers a series of options from which to construct a lesson. Both student and teacher can choose as much or as little support as you like.

The 'Problems'

What's the simplest way to use *Decisionmaker*?

Choose a 'problem', read it with your students and then discuss a solution. At the end of each 'problem', you'll find a 'free discussion' question which the discussion should attempt to answer.

The units are arranged in no particular order – so use the Contents page and the 'At A Glance' section at the beginning of the Teacher's pages to choose the problem that most interests you and your learners.

If you and your learners want more support, the book also offers a range of support material which you may choose to use in conjunction with the problem. Here are the options:

Options for the student

Before you read

Before the students read the problem itself, they can:
• Read the 'Background Box' for background information on the problem
• Try the 'Way In' activity as an introduction to the theme of the problem

Word file

As the students read the problem, they can refer to this section for help with vocabulary.
Note: The explanations provided are not the kind of definitions that you would find in a dictionary. They explain what the word or phrase means in the particular context of the problem.

Analysis

The analysis section normally takes the student through the problem paragraph by paragraph. When the students have read the paragraph, they refer to the analysis section and are asked a question or invited to take part in an activity.

Decision time

This section offers the student a way of structuring their thoughts as they attempt to solve the problem.

All sections for the learner are photocopiable.

For the teacher

This section contains the following:

At a glance

This sums up the key points of the unit, to help you choose the right one for you and your learners.

Answers

This section gives answers, where appropriate, to questions in the 'Before You Read', 'Analysis' and 'Decision time' sections. There are often no "right" answers to the questions asked, as many of them are intended to promote discussion rather than to test. However, as a guide, this section suggests answers to most questions.

Summary

This is a summary of the main points for your reference during the discussion.

Suggested activity

In some of the units, there is a suggestion for a way of structuring the class discussion.

A follow-up activity

Some units have extra activities which will allow you to do some additional work on the theme of the central problem.

A possible solution

There are no right or wrong solutions to these problems, but your learners may like to compare their conclusions with the author's idea for a solution.

Procedure

If you chose to use all the options in a unit, your lesson would probably
follow this sequence:

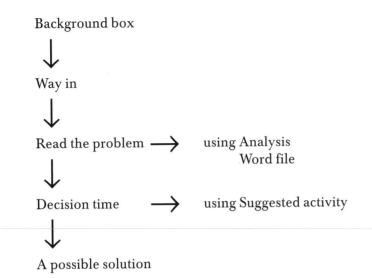

Background box

Way in

Read the problem ⟶ using Analysis Word file

Decision time ⟶ using Suggested activity

A possible solution

But, remember, you don't have to use all these options – choose the ones
that are appropriate for your needs.

A note on feedback

The main aim of this book is to promote discussion. However, learners
may find it helpful to receive some feedback on their effectiveness and
accuracy in the use of language. If you decide to provide this, it's probably
best to take notes during the discussions and to present your feedback at
the end of the session. If you continually interrupt the class, learners will
probably find it difficult to concentrate on the task itself!

Smoke Signals

Before you read

'Smoke Signals' is set in the world of cigarette marketing. If you'd like to find out something about the trends in this market, read this background box:

Background

> ### The world tobacco market
>
> As people have become increasingly aware of the health risks, consumption of cigarettes has fallen in Western Europe and North America. This has meant that big tobacco companies have started looking elsewhere for promising new markets. The result has been a steady increase in the number of smokers in Asia, Africa and the countries of the former Soviet Union.

Way in

When people choose a career, they often have to make a choice between looking after their own interests and trying to help others. The following matrix is a way of looking at the relationship between making money and doing good in society.

The jobs matrix

Doctors make a lot of money and are good for society, so they are placed in the top right quadrant. Pickpockets don't do any good for society and they (normally) don't make much money either, so they go in the bottom left quadrant.

Lots of money	*Doctor*
Not much money *Pick-pocket*	

Bad for society　　　**Good for society**

Where in the matrix would you put these jobs?

soldier
drug dealer
financial speculator
car salesperson
nurse
politician

Decisionmaker
Smoke Signals

© Cambridge
University Press
1997

Smoke Signals

Problem

Kim Jin Hiu had never touched a cigarette in her life, but when Jean Nicot Tobacco Inc offered her a job, she didn't hesitate. The US-based Jean Nicot Corporation was one of the world's oldest and largest tobacco manufacturers and it was offering the 23-year-old South Korean woman the chance of a lifetime. As one of its elite marketing trainees, Jin Hiu could look forward to a generous salary, fantastic fringe benefits and a jet-set lifestyle that would be the envy of her friends.

Of course, there was some opposition to her taking the job. Her father didn't like the idea of his daughter working for a foreign company. Her mother and brother were more worried about the health aspects of the tobacco industry. 'You're persuading people to kill themselves,' her brother told her.

But Jin Hiu had looked into the ethics of cigarette marketing while she was at business school and her conscience was clear. She accepted the argument that cigarette advertising did not try to get more people to smoke, it simply encouraged existing smokers to change brands. After all, smokers were adults who were responsible for their own actions. Her role as a marketing professional was not to mislead or to manipulate: it was to help the public to make informed choices.

During her initial three-month training course at Nicot's headquarters in New Orleans, Jin Hiu's attitudes and enthusiasm impressed the company's senior executives and she was seen as a potential high-flier. In recognition of this, they asked her to present a paper at the end of her course. Its theme was to be 'New Opportunities in the Korean cigarette market.'

Jin Hiu spent much of her free time researching her paper in the company library. One afternoon, while working through a stack of documents, she came across a file marked 'S. Korea/Strictly Confidential/for Board level only'. She realised that she had been given it by mistake and she knew that she shouldn't read its contents. But, she couldn't resist taking a quick look.

Word file

elite marketing trainee	a talented person employed by a company and trained to become a marketing specialist
fringe benefits	rewards given to an employee in addition to his/her salary
jet-set	a group of rich, glamorous people who travel a lot
ethics	moral beliefs
her conscience was clear	she didn't feel worried or guilty
to manipulate	to make people do what you want them to do
informed choices	choices based on good information
high-flier	a clever person who will probably be a great success
to present a paper	to give a presentation
a stack of documents	a pile of papers
For Board Level Only	only to be read by the most senior people in a company

Decisionmaker
Smoke Signals

© Cambridge
University Press
1997

This is what she found:

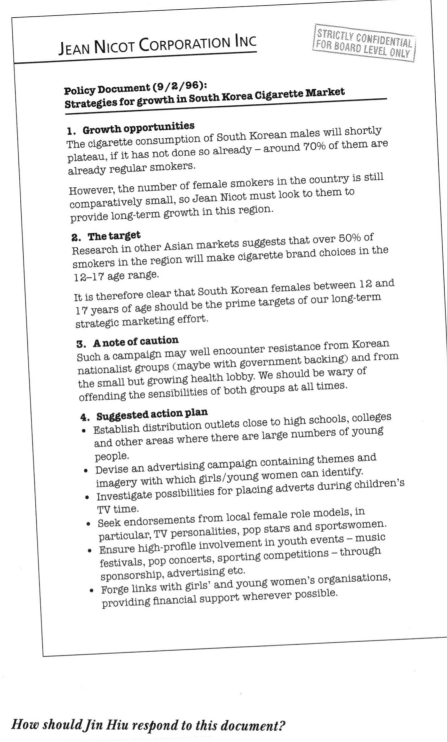

JEAN NICOT CORPORATION INC

STRICTLY CONFIDENTIAL FOR BOARD LEVEL ONLY

**Policy Document (9/2/96):
Strategies for growth in South Korea Cigarette Market**

1. Growth opportunities
The cigarette consumption of South Korean males will shortly plateau, if it has not done so already – around 70% of them are already regular smokers.

However, the number of female smokers in the country is still comparatively small, so Jean Nicot must look to them to provide long-term growth in this region.

2. The target
Research in other Asian markets suggests that over 50% of smokers in the region will make cigarette brand choices in the 12–17 age range.

It is therefore clear that South Korean females between 12 and 17 years of age should be the prime targets of our long-term strategic marketing effort.

3. A note of caution
Such a campaign may well encounter resistance from Korean nationalist groups (maybe with government backing) and from the small but growing health lobby. We should be wary of offending the sensibilities of both groups at all times.

4. Suggested action plan
- Establish distribution outlets close to high schools, colleges and other areas where there are large numbers of young people.
- Devise an advertising campaign containing themes and imagery with which girls/young women can identify.
- Investigate possibilities for placing adverts during children's TV time.
- Seek endorsements from local female role models, in particular, TV personalities, pop stars and sportswomen.
- Ensure high-profile involvement in youth events – music festivals, pop concerts, sporting competitions – through sponsorship, advertising etc.
- Forge links with girls' and young women's organisations, providing financial support wherever possible.

Free discussion

How should Jin Hiu respond to this document?

Word file

consumption	buying
to plateau	to level off
cigarette brand choice	the decision to buy a particular type of cigarette
prime targets	a company's most important future customers
strategic marketing effort	a long-term plan to make people buy a company's products
health lobby	a group of people who persuade others to have a healthier lifestyle
to offend sensibilities	to hurt or insult feelings
endorsement	an agreement to write your name on a product
role models	people whose behaviour is copied by others
sponsorship	financial support provided by a person or organisation
to forge links	to establish a connection or a relationship

Decisionmaker
Smoke Signals

© Cambridge University Press 1997

Analysis

Paragraph 1: The chance of a lifetime?
Read the first paragraph, turn to the jobs matrix (in the 'Way in' section) and then think about these questions:
a) Where would you put Jin Hiu's job in the jobs matrix?
b) Would you accept the job if you were in her position?

Paragraph 2: Should she take the job?
After reading the second paragraph, divide into pairs and try this role play:
One member of each pair should try to explain why Jin Hiu should accept the job, the other why she shouldn't. (If you like, you can play the roles of Jin Hiu and her brother in this discussion.)

Paragraph 3: Cigarette adverts
Read the third paragraph and then look at this fact:

> Cigarette advertising was banned in Italy in 1962, but since then cigarette consumption has increased by 30% per person.

Now discuss this issue:
Do you agree with Jin Hiu? Do cigarette advertisements only try to persuade smokers to change brands, or do they have other objectives? If so, what are they?
If you did the 'Jobs matrix' activity, go back to it and think about this point:
Where do you think that Jin Hiu would put her job in the jobs matrix?

Paragraphs 4 and 5: What would you do?
When you've read paragraphs 4 and 5, think about this question:
If you were in Jin Hiu's position and found a top secret document, would you read it?

The policy document
Approach the policy document in this way:
A quick scan: Don't read the document in detail – scan it as fast as possible and try to find the answer to this question:
Which group of people is the main target for Jean Nicot's long-term marketing strategy?
The suggested action plan: Look at the ideas in this plan and think about/discuss these questions:
1 Do you think that these ideas will help to improve Jean Nicot's sales in South Korea? Which ones will be most effective?
2 Do you think that any of the ideas are morally wrong? If so, explain why.
Overall: Is the strategy in this document compatible with Jin Hiu's views on her role as a cigarette marketer? (Her views are explained in paragraph 3.) Give reasons to support your answer.

Now, move on to make your decision!

Decisionmaker
Smoke Signals

© Cambridge
University Press
1997

The decision

Decision time

How should Jin Hiu respond to the policy document?

Try thinking about the problem in this way:

Self-interest or morals?

Should Jin Hiu look after her own interests? Or should she respond to the problem in a moral way?

Look at this list of options and decide which ones are self-interested responses and which are moral responses to the issue:

	Self-interested response?	Moral response?
• ignore it	*ignore it*	
• photocopy the document and give it to the newspapers		
• resign from the company		
• use it as the basis for your paper		
• stay with the company but fight against the policy		
• discuss the policy with a senior manager		

Now decide!

Which response would you choose?
Does Jin Hiu have any other options in this situation?

Decisionmaker
Smoke Signals

© Cambridge
University Press
1997

At a glance

Topic:	Cigarettes, marketing, business ethics
New vocabulary:	Marketing
Scenario:	A young marketing trainee discovers that her cigarette company is planning to focus its home marketing strategy on teenage girls in her home country.
Additional background information:	Jean Nicot's marketing plan might sound outrageous, but some cigarette companies have undoubtedly targeted children in their marketing strategies. A leaked memo from a Canadian tobacco company listed teenagers as a target group, and cigarette adverts are regularly shown on children's TV in Japan. In 1991, a study showed that American children as young as six could identify Joe Camel (a cartoon character advertising Camel cigarettes) as easily as Mickey Mouse!

Answers

Way in (*suggested answers*)

```
               Financial speculator

Lots of    Drug dealer        Doctor
money                         Politician

               ───Car salesperson───

Not
much       Pick-pocket        Soldier
money                         Nurse


          Bad for society   Good for society
```

Analysis

Paragraphs 1 and 3
You decide!

The policy document
A quick scan: South Korean girls between the ages of 12 and 17.

The suggested action plan: The answers here are purely a matter of opinion. Students must decide for themselves.

Overall: The strategy is not compatible with Jin Hiu's ideas, for these reasons:

- She believed that the purpose of cigarette advertising was to make people change brands, not to make them start smoking.

- She thought that Jean Nicot would be selling cigarettes to adults, not children.
- Some of these ideas do not help consumers make informed choices, they are clearly designed to manipulate (e.g. use of female role models).

Decision time

Self-interest or morals? (*suggested answers*)

Self-interested responses: ignore it; use it as the basis for your paper; discuss the policy with a senior manager.

Moral responses: photocopy the document and give it to the newspapers; resign from the company; stay with the company but fight against the policy.

Summary

The decisionmaker	**Kim Jin Hiu**
The decision	**How should she respond to the contents of the policy document?**
The issues	**1 Is Jean Nicot's policy acceptable in any way?**
	2 Should Jin Hiu look after her own career or take a moral stand on this issue?
	3 Should Jin Hiu try to hide the fact that she's read the document?

Suggested activity: Camps of opinion

In this activity students seek out others who share their views about what Jin Hiu should and should not do in this situation. It provides a chance to practise ways of expressing opinion (In my opinion, Jin Hiu should do this, Jean Nicot shouldn't do that, etc.).

1 Using the six options set out in the 'Self-interest or morals?' activity, ask the students to work alone and choose the best thing and the worst thing that Jin Hiu could do in this situation.

2 Get the students to walk around the classroom looking for people who have chosen the same two options. With a bit of luck you should soon find 'camps' of like-minded people developing.

3 Ask each 'camp' to prepare a brief statement justifying its collective view and to state whether it thinks its views are self-interested, moral or balanced.

4 Have a general class discussion on the views of each group.

Broadening the discussion

Should cigarette companies be allowed to advertise? If so, what restrictions should be placed on their advertising? If not, should cigarettes be banned totally?

A possible solution

There is no suggested solution to this unit: it's a matter for each individual's conscience.

Follow-up activity

Using the information in this unit, get the students to devise a marketing strategy and/or advertising campaign designed to persuade teenagers not to smoke.

A Pirate's Dilemma

Before you read

This problem concerns the illegal copying of video tapes. If you want to find out more about 'piracy' and the protection of ideas, read this background box:

Background

> **Intellectual property**
>
> The illegal copying, or 'pirating', of products like books, music recordings, videos and computer software is big business throughout the world. It is, of course, extremely difficult to protect products like these, because they are based on ideas, but there are many international agreements which try to do so – including the 1993 Gatt trade agreement.
>
> But so far, these efforts have not had a great effect. The United States estimates that in 1993 piracy cost its businesses over $8 billion.

The problem also raises some questions about business ethics. To think about business ethics in a general way, try this 'Way in' activity:

Way in

Imagine that each member of your group has been given $100. Each person must choose to divide this money between 'private' and 'public' accounts. At the end of the activity you keep the money in your private account; however, the total amount of money in the public account will be doubled and then redistributed equally among all members of the group.

Do not discuss the problem, but write down the way in which you have chosen to divide your money (e.g. 50 public:50 private; 20 public:80 private, etc.) and hand in your papers to your group leader. The group leader then works out how much money should be redistributed and announces the result.

Now, add the redistributed money to the money in your private accounts and find out how much each person in the group has.

Discuss the following points:
1 Why did you choose to divide the $100 as you did?
2 What was the best course of action:
   • for the group as a whole?
   • for each individual?
3 What role did ethics play in your decisions?

Decisionmaker
A Pirate's Dilemma

© Cambridge University Press 1997

A Pirate's Dilemma

Problem

If you wanted to see a good movie in south-east Moscow, the place to go was Tatiana Belova's kiosk. Her kiosk contained all the top Hollywood films, available for sale very cheaply – and she would often have the latest box-office hit before it arrived in Russian cinemas.

'How do you do it, Tatiana?' her customers often asked her.

'Ah, it's no secret,' she would say, 'Tom Cruise is a personal friend of mine.'

That always made them laugh. The 55-year-old grandmother was the last person you could imagine socialising with anyone from Hollywood's jet set.

In fact, Tatiana's supplies of videos were delivered every month by a man in a black Mercedes. They came in plain white boxes, with their titles neatly typed on the sides. Of course, Tatiana guessed that the man had a few connections in Moscow's underworld, but she knew better than to ask unnecessary questions. Besides, his prices were reasonable and for a small extra fee, he made sure that nothing bad happened to her kiosk at night.

Tatiana considered herself to be an honest woman. She didn't cheat her customers, she settled her bills promptly – she even paid her taxes! But one morning, she arrived at her kiosk to find a letter that made her think:

Word file

kiosk	a small hut with a large window at the front, often used in the former Soviet Union as a shop
video library	a collection of films on video cassette
box-office hit	a film that is a great financial success at cinemas
Tom Cruise	one of Hollywood's top actors
to socialise	to mix with other people for pleasure
jet set	a group of rich, glamorous people who travel a lot
underworld	criminal society
to cheat	to deceive
promptly	quickly

Decisionmaker
A Pirate's Dilemma

© Cambridge University Press 1997

Borodino Distributors
Box 36954
Moscow

Dear Mrs Belova,

As I'm sure you know, selling pirated copies of films is a serious crime under international law.

Every time someone watches a film that has been illegally copied, it means that the artists who made that film are working for nothing. Their talent and their hard work has been stolen. Even worse, video piracy is threatening the existence of the film industry itself. After all, if everybody in the world pirated movies, there would be no film industry and no new movies for anybody to enjoy!

Our organisation represents many of Hollywood's major studios, and we are currently offering a number of small businesses in the Moscow area the chance to become official distributors of our videos.

As an official distributor, you will be able to sell top-quality versions of all the latest video releases, in their original packaging. You will also be able to use our own publicity material to promote both our films and your business.

We are confident that you will recognise this as the perfect opportunity to prepare your business for the challenges of the next millennium. One of our representatives will be calling on you later in the week to discuss the matter further.

Yours sincerely

V. N. Stellovsky

V. N. Stellovsky

She put down the letter and roared with laughter. Imagine – Tatiana in her little kiosk doing business with a representative of Hollywood! Her friend in the black Mercedes would have a good laugh about that!

But as she trudged back through the snow to her apartment that evening, she started to give Borodino's proposal some more serious thought…

Free discussion

What should Tatiana say to Borodino's representative when he visits her later in the week?

Word file

video releases	films available on video cassette
the next millennium	the thousand years beginning at the year 2000
studio	a film production company (often these companies are also responsible for many other functions such as marketing, distribution, etc.)
to trudge	to walk slowly and with difficulty

Decisionmaker
A Pirate's Dilemma

© Cambridge University Press 1997

Analysis

Paragraph 1: Do you believe it?

Read the first paragraph and decide which of these sentences are true and which are false:

1 Tatiana owned a cinema in Moscow.
2 She had videos of all the top Russian movies.
3 She could get the most successful Hollywood films before they arrived in the Russian cinemas.
4 Tom Cruise is a personal friend of Tatiana.

Paragraph 2: The man in the black Mercedes

Read the paragraph and answer these questions:

1 Why do you think that the videos come in white boxes with their titles typed on the side?
2 Why doesn't Tatiana ask unnecessary questions?
3 What extra service does the man offer?

Paragraph 3: An honest woman?

Read the paragraph and then discuss this question:
Would you say that Tatiana was an honest woman?

The letter

Scan the letter from Borodino and answer these three questions:

1 What are the arguments against video piracy?
2 What is Borodino offering?
3 What are the practical advantages of the offer?

Now, discuss these points:

1 According to some reports, in the early 1990s Tom Cruise could earn over $12 million for one movie. At the same time, the average monthly salary of a teacher at Moscow State University was just $100. So why should ordinary Russians worry about the earnings of Hollywood stars?
2 For Tatiana, does Borodino's offer sound like an attractive business proposal?

Read to the end of the story and then move on to discuss your decision.

Decisionmaker
**A Pirate's
Dilemma**

© Cambridge
University Press
1997

The decision

Decision time

Should Tatiana continue to sell pirate videos, or should she accept the offer to become an official video distributor?

From a show of hands, find out which people support which alternative. Then try this activity:

Devil's advocate

When discussing ethical problems, people often immediately have strongly-held opinions. So, to think round the problem, try playing 'devil's advocate'. A devil's advocate tests an opinion by arguing for the opposite case as strongly as possible, even if he or she doesn't believe in what s/he's saying.

Take a few minutes to think of a few arguments which justify the opinion that is the <u>opposite</u> of your own. Then find another member of the group who has prepared a set of arguments which oppose yours, and argue with him or her as fiercely as you can! (NB: Both members of each pair should be arguing for the cases that they <u>don't</u> believe in.)

When you've looked at both sides of the problem from an ethical point of view, think about the practical implications of the possible decisions, with this exercise:

Worst case scenarios

In pairs or small groups, think about the worst things that could possibly happen to Tatiana, by discussing these two questions:

1 What might the man in the black Mercedes do if Tatiana accepts Borodino's offer?
2 What might Borodino do if she doesn't?

Now divide into pairs and try this role play. One person plays Tatiana and the other plays Borodino's representative.

Role play

What should Tatiana say to Borodino's representative when he visits her later in the week?

Now decide!

Again from a show of hands, find out which members of the group support which option and see how many people have changed their minds as a result of your discussions. What should Tatiana do?

Decisionmaker
A Pirate's Dilemma

© Cambridge University Press 1997

At a glance

Topic:	Video piracy, business ethics
New vocabulary:	Film/video industry, distribution
Scenario:	A Russian video pirate is offered the chance to become an official video distributor.

Answers

Way in

Clearly the best course of action for *the group as a whole* is for everybody to put all their money into the public account. However, for *each individual*, the best course of action will probably be to put all the money into the private account – because they will still receive their share of everybody else's money from the public account (assuming, of course, that everybody else doesn't have the same idea!).

Analysis

Paragraph 1: Do you believe it?
1 false   2 false   3 true   4 false

Paragraph 2: The man in the black Mercedes
1 Because they're illegal copies.
2 Because the man has connections with the criminal underworld.
3 Protection: he makes sure that nothing bad happens to her kiosk at night.

The letter
1 It's a crime under international law; people who make films are not getting the payment they deserve; it's threatening the existence of the film industry.
2 The chance to become an official distributor of videos.
3 Top quality videos, original packaging, publicity material and selling videos legally rather than illegally.

Summary

The decisionmaker	Tatiana Belova
The decision	Should Tatiana continue to sell pirate videos or should she accept the offer to become an official video distributor?
The issues	1 Is it more important to pursue self-interest (sell pirate videos) or to act for the common good (become an official distributor)?
	2 What are the implications of the two alternatives for Tatiana's business?
	3 If she continues to sell pirate videos, what will Borodino do?
	4 If she accepts Borodino's offer, what will the man in the black Mercedes do?

A possible solution

The important decision here is the ethical one – whether to continue to sell pirate videos or to accept Borodino's offer. That is clearly a matter for each individual's conscience. However, even in taking a moral decision such as this one Tatiana should also consider the other factors at work. In particular, she needs to think how her 'friend' in the black Mercedes will react. As he is providing her not just with pirate video tapes but also with 'protection', she should assess the possible risks both to herself and to her business if she chooses to accept Borodino's offer.

Follow-up discussion

Is Borodino's strategy a good way of coping with the problem of video piracy? What other ways are there of dealing with it?

A Year in Fashion

Before you read

This story is set in a fashion house. To find out some background about the world of fashion, read this background box:

Background

> **Fashion houses**
>
> Fashion houses are companies which design and sell small quantities of very expensive and fashionable clothes – a few well-known examples are Giorgio Armani, Comme des Garçons and Paul Smith.
>
> Normally, these companies don't actually produce the clothes themselves. They are often too small to have their own factories, and the demands of the fashion business mean that they have to continually change their designs, so it is difficult for them to organise mass production. As a result, fashion houses are not always in total control of their costs and can suffer from sudden changes in market conditions.

This story looks at problems caused when borrowing money. If you'd like to think about the ethics of money lending, discuss this point:

Way in

The lending of money in return for interest is a central feature of capitalism. However, people have always been very critical of money lending, not least because it seems as if money lenders get paid without having to do any work. So, what is the justification for banks charging interest on their loans?

Decisionmaker
A Year in Fashion

© Cambridge University Press 1997

A Year in Fashion

Problem

With her own thriving London fashion house, Suzanne Fernet appeared to be one of the most successful and confident people in the fashion business. But did the entries in her private diary tell a different story?

27 May

Just back from our selling show in Paris. I always had a good feeling about this spring collection, but this was better than I ever imagined: orders from our wholesale customers are up by over 50% on last year. The Far Eastern buyers, in particular, have gone crazy about us – at this rate, we'll have half the women in Tokyo wearing a Suzanne Fernet dress!

May Week No. 22

6 June

Meeting with the bank manager this morning. He went a bit white when I talked him through the summer's business plan, but I think he sees what we're trying to do. The big orders mean that our outgoings have shot up – extra staff in the office, the cost of fabric, production costs and so on – and we won't see any return for all this until the wholesalers start paying us in the autumn. The result is that we need a huge (I mean huge!) increase in our overdraft. He agreed to it reluctantly, but he insisted on a review in September.

June Week No. 23

abc

Word file

thriving	very busy and successful
fashion house	a company that designs and sells fashionable clothes
spring collection	a range of clothes specially designed for the spring season (NB: in this case, the clothes will not be in the shops until the year following the showing of the collection)
wholesale customers	customers who buy goods in large quantities and sell them on to other businesses
to go white	to look nervous or afraid
outgoings	money spent by a business
to shoot up	to increase very quickly
fabric	the material from which clothes are made
overdraft	a loan made by a bank that allows the customer to have a negative balance in their account

Decisionmaker
A Year in Fashion

© Cambridge University Press 1997

18 August

Gloomy reading in the newspapers. Interest rates in this country are going up again (which means that my overdraft will start costing an arm and a leg!) and there's talk of recession in Japan. Still, there's no point in worrying. Our producers have done the work and been paid, and most of the orders have been shipped. So, all we can do is to sit and wait for the money to start coming in.

August   Week No. 33

11 September

Bad news. I had a meeting with Angie, one of my credit controllers, this morning. Apparently, our biggest Japanese customer is having serious financial problems. Angie says that they want to pay for their order in instalments, and that if we push them for the whole payment now, she's worried that they'll go out of business and we'll get nothing. I don't know what the bank manager will say about that!

15 September

Awful meeting with the bank manager. I wanted the overdraft to be extended; he insists that we reduce it immediately. I pleaded and pleaded with him, but he just won't budge. He wants to see us taking some action now, he said.

So, what are my options?

1 We slash the costs of our operation – lay off staff, sell equipment, scale back our plans for next year. That would certainly bring the overdraft down – but what about the future of my business?

2 We agree to let our Japanese customer pay in instalments, so at least we get some money from them now. That should keep the bank manager happy. But that means that until I receive the final instalment, I'm offering them free credit, while running a huge overdraft myself!

3 We demand payment in full from the Japanese – and run the risk of them going out of business.

4 I find the money that I need from another source. Do I apply for another loan from another bank? Do I borrow from friends? Or even re-mortgage my house?

September   Week No. 36

Free discussion

What is Suzanne's best option?

Word file

gloomy	depressing
to cost an arm and a leg	to cost a lot of money
recession	a period of reduction in business activity
to ship	to deliver to a customer in another country
credit controller	a person responsible for collecting money owed to a business
instalments	a series of payments
to extend	to go beyond an agreed limit
to plead	to ask for something in a desperate way
to budge	to change your position
to slash	to reduce dramatically
to lay off	to dismiss people from work in order to reduce costs
to scale back	to reduce
to re-mortgage	to use your house to guarantee a loan

Analysis

At the end of each entry stop and answer the relevant questions:

27 May: Get the facts straight

1 Where was the selling show?   2 What was being sold?

3 Which buyers in particular liked her collection?

4 Was the show successful?

6 June: Getting the money

1 Why did the bank manager go white?

   a) Because of the extra staff in Suzanne's office.

   b) Because Suzanne's got such big orders.

   c) Because Suzanne wants a big overdraft.

2 Why have Suzanne's outgoings shot up?

   a) Because of the extra staff, the cost of extra fabric, and higher production costs, all needed to meet the big orders.

   b) Because the wholesalers will pay in the autumn.

   c) Because of the huge increase in Suzanne's overdraft.

18 August: Why gloomy?

1 Why is the rise in interest rates bad news for Suzanne?

2 What's the problem with a recession in Japan?

11 September: The risks

1 Why is Angie worried about asking the Japanese for the full payment now?

2 Why is it not in Suzanne's interests to receive the payment in instalments?

15 September: A letter from the bank

When you've read the first paragraph of this entry, read this letter from the bank summarising the meeting, and fill in the gaps using the words underneath:

Dear Ms Fernet

Further to our .... yesterday, I confirm that we are unable to extend your .... on its current terms. Indeed, we urgently request that you take action to .... your level of indebtedness immediately.

When we see that you are taking appropriate ...., we will be only too happy to .... further overdraft requirements.

Let me assure you that you remain a valued .... of our branch.

Yours sincerely

| overdraft | meeting | customer | reduce | discuss | action |

Now, read Suzanne's four options and then move on to make your decision!

Decisionmaker
A Year in Fashion

© Cambridge University Press 1997

The decision

Decision time

How can Suzanne reduce her overdraft?

Paired comparisons

Here is a technique which helps you to compare all four different options with each other. Begin by comparing the advantages and disadvantages of options 1 and 2, and then write your preferred option in the box. Then do the same with options 1 and 3. Continue until you've filled all six empty boxes with your preferences. Then see which option has been chosen most often.

	1 Slash costs	2 Pay in instalments	3 Demand full payment	4 Another source?
1 Slash costs				
2 Pay in instalments				
3 Demand full payment				

Are there any alternatives?

When you've done the paired comparison exercise, discuss:
1 Are there any other options that Suzanne hasn't thought of?
2 Is there a compromise that she should consider?

Now decide!

What action should Suzanne take?

Decisionmaker
A Year in Fashion

© Cambridge University Press 1997

At a glance

Topic:	Fashion, credit control
New vocabulary:	Fashion
Scenario:	Late payment for an order threatens the survival of a small fashion house.

Answers

Way in

There are many justifications for the charging of interest on loans – here are two:

- Interest compensates the lender for the risk that the loan will not be repaid.
- Interest ensures that the value of the loan (to the lender) will not be reduced by inflation.

Analysis

27 May: Get the facts straight

1 Paris
2 Suzanne Fernet's spring collection
3 Buyers from the Far East, Japan, in particular
4 Yes, orders from wholesale customers were up 50% on the previous year.

6 June: Getting the money

1 c)
2 b)

18 August: Why gloomy?

1 Because the interest payments on her overdraft will increase.
2 Because many of her customers are Japanese.

11 September: The risks

1 In case they go out of business and Suzanne receives nothing.
2 Because Suzanne needs the money now to repay her overdraft.

15 September: A letter from the bank

1 meeting   2 overdraft   3 reduce
4 action   5 discuss   6 customer

Summary

The decisionmaker	Suzanne Fernet
The decision	How can Suzanne reduce her overdraft?
The issues	1 Which of the four options should she choose?
	2 Is there a compromise or an option that has not been considered?

A possible solution

There's nothing wrong with Suzanne's business – apart from her current cash flow problem. If she can overcome this, she should have a great future, which means that option 1 would be a terrible mistake. Option 3 is too risky – if the Japanese customer goes out of business and cannot pay her, she'll be in terrible difficulties. Although it seems stupid to pay for an overdraft only to offer free credit to one of your customers, option 2 is probably the best solution. If for any reason that fails, option 4 would be her last resort.

Follow-up activity

Write a letter from Suzanne to her bank manager, explaining the decision you've taken.

Big Fish Don't Jump

Before you read

This story is set in the business worlds of China and Hong Kong. To find out more read this background box:

Background

China and Hong Kong

With a population of over 1.2 billion people, China is potentially the biggest market in the world. Since its government first introduced free market reforms in 1978, its economy has grown at an incredible rate. Look at the city of Shenzen (mentioned in this unit): between 1984 and 1994 its population grew from 320,000 to 2.5 million people, while its industrial production grew by over 60% each year.

But there are still big differences between China and Hong Kong. Under the administration of the British government until 1997, the city of Hong Kong developed into a showcase of Asian capitalism and by 1993 was considered to be the sixth richest country in the world.

Way in

Business decisions should be based on hard facts, but rumour and reputation often have a very big part to play, too.

Imagine that you are planning to buy a house. Which of these factors would have the biggest negative effect on your decision to buy? Rank them from most negative (1) to least negative (6).

Factor	Rank
A broken window	☐
A rumour that a man had been murdered there fifty years ago	☐
A neighbour playing a loud electric guitar	☐
A story that the seller has a criminal record	☐
A strange smell in the bathroom	☐
Tasteless decorations in the main room	☐

Discuss whether your decisions are based more on hard fact or rumour and reputation.

Decisionmaker
**Big Fish
Don't Jump**

© Cambridge
University Press
1997

Big Fish Don't Jump

Problem

At the press conference to announce his latest hotel construction project, Hong Kong businessman Alan Peng was in a particularly good mood.

'I can guarantee,' he told his audience, 'that this will be the finest new hotel in downtown Shenzen. And it will be ready for its first occupants in less than two years.'

Several of the journalists looked up from their notebooks. 'Are you serious about that deadline?' asked one of them.

'Like I said,' Alan Peng replied, 'I guarantee it.' Then he paused and roared with laughter. 'I'll tell you what. If it's late… if it's late, I'll dive into Victoria Harbour.'

The conference broke up with the journalists still laughing at the idea of the millionaire tycoon jumping into Hong Kong's busiest and most polluted stretch of water.

Twenty months later, Alan Peng didn't find his joke quite so funny, when his aide, Harry Selig, handed him an article from one of Hong Kong's business journals:

BIG FISH DON'T JUMP

Alan Peng runs into problems on mainland China

by Nancy Au in Hong Kong

Alan Peng might be a big fish in the small pond of Hong Kong business, but when it comes to working on mainland China, he is a fish out of water.

At the beginning of last year, Peng boasted that he could build Shenzen's finest luxury hotel in record time. But after a series of disputes with contractors and botched negotiations with officials, the hotel looks like being neither Shenzen's finest, nor ready anywhere near its promised completion date.

A spokesman for Peng's company, Peng Holdings, claimed that the delays were due to the intransigence of local planning authorities. However, industry insiders are saying that Peng's cost-cutting measures and insensitive management have brought the project to the brink of standstill. The news comes at a bad time for Peng Holdings. Rumours have been flying around the Hong Kong Stock Exchange that Peng's investment in a Shanghai-based plastics factory has also turned sour and that his company is now desperately short of liquidity.

So, is there any chance of the Shenzen hotel meeting its two year completion deadline? When Alan Peng announced the project, he promised that if the hotel was not completed on time, he would dive into Hong Kong's Victoria Harbour. As his financial backers will soon find out, when it comes to keeping his promises, Alan Peng is a big fish who just doesn't jump.

Decisionmaker
Big Fish Don't Jump

© Cambridge University Press 1997

'Shall I ask our lawyers to do something about this?' asked Selig.

'I don't know, Harry,' said Peng. 'A long court case is not going to help us. This is a question of confidence. It's true that we're not going to meet the deadline on the Shenzen hotel, but we still need to show people that we mean what we say.'

Peng walked over to the window and looked out across the Hong Kong skyline.

Harry Selig watched his boss and tried to read his thoughts. 'Alan,' he said, 'you're not thinking of… Alan, listen, you're fifty-five years old. You're one of the most respected businessmen in this city. Alan, please, don't…'

But Alan Peng wasn't listening.

Free discussion

How should Alan Peng respond to the article?

Word file

press conference	a meeting arranged to give a statement to journalists and answer questions
deadline	the time by which something should be completed
Victoria Harbour	Hong Kong's busiest waterway. (Although it's polluted, diving into it probably wouldn't be very dangerous. But it wouldn't be a pleasant experience!)
tycoon	a rich and powerful business person
aide	an assistant to an important person
a big fish in a small pond	someone who is important in a comparatively unimportant place
Hong Kong/mainland China	here Hong Kong refers to the 236 islands which make up the (former) British colony; mainland China refers to the main part of the People's Republic of China
a fish out of water	someone who is uncomfortable because s/he is in an unfamiliar situation
contractors	independent companies which sign contracts to do part of a bigger job
botched negotiations	negotiations which have failed because they have been badly handled
promised completion date	the date by which the work should be done
intransigence	refusal to change an opinion or negotiating position
local planning authorities	government organisations that allow buildings to be built or altered
industry insiders	people with special or secret knowledge of a particular industry
the brink of standstill	the edge of stopping completely
to turn sour	to go bad
liquidity	the state of having cash or assets that can be easily turned into cash
financial backers	people who have invested money in something
court case	legal hearing

Decisionmaker
**Big Fish
Don't Jump**

© Cambridge
University Press
1997

Analysis

The press conference

Quick quiz
Quickly scan the first paragraph and find the answers to these four questions:
1 What did Alan Peng announce at the press conference?
2 Where is Alan Peng based?
3 When will the project be completed?
4 What does Alan Peng say he will do if the project is not finished before the deadline?

The article

Paragraph 1: Idioms
The opening paragraph is based on two English idioms: 'a big fish in a small pond', and 'a fish out of water'.
In this context, what is 'the small pond'? And where is 'out of water'?

Paragraphs 2–4: Check the facts
Journalists can't write things which are untrue – if they do they could face legal action. But unfortunately, they don't always have time to check all their facts thoroughly. Because of this, they often use techniques which allow them to tell the story without saying that it is all <u>definitely</u> true.

Imagine that you're a lawyer and read paragraphs 2–4 very carefully. Then decide which of the following statements are <u>definitely</u> true and which <u>might</u> be true, according to the paper:
1 Alan Peng definitely said that he could build the hotel in record time.
2 The hotel will definitely not be ready before its deadline.
3 Delays in the construction project were definitely due to the intransigence of planning authorities.
4 Alan Peng's cost-cutting and insensitive management have definitely stopped the project.
5 Another of Alan Peng's investments has definitely gone bad.

In these paragraphs, which of these words or phrases tell you that some of the statements are <u>not</u> definitely true?

neither … nor	however,
looks like	industry insiders are saying
claimed	rumours
intransigence	desperately

Read his thoughts

Now read to the end of the problem and then discuss this question:
What thoughts are going through Alan Peng's mind as he stares out over Hong Kong?

Now, move on to make your decision.

Decisionmaker
**Big Fish
Don't Jump**

© Cambridge
University Press
1997

The decision

Decision time

What should Alan Peng do?

Try thinking about the problem in this way:

Define and restate

When you're solving problems, it's important to think clearly and to avoid becoming confused by details. To help them do this, businesspeople often follow the process of 'Define and restate'. Discuss each stage in this process.

1 Is there really a problem?

Firstly, decide if Alan Peng is really facing a problem – perhaps he has nothing to worry about!

2 If there is a problem, what exactly is it?

Here are four ideas: Peng's problem could be one of these things, a combination of them, or something completely different. What do you think?

- The rumours at the stock exchange
- Alan Peng's promise to jump into the harbour
- The delay in the hotel project
- How to respond to the journalist's article

3 Re-state the problem in your own words:

Alan Peng's problem is ....

....

....

Now decide!

When you've agreed on a definition and restatement of the problem, you should find it much easier to agree on a solution.

Decisionmaker
**Big Fish
Don't Jump**

© Cambridge
University Press
1997

At a glance

Topic:	Business credibility
New vocabulary:	Property development, newspapers
Scenario:	The reputation of a top Hong Kong businessman is attacked in a newspaper article.

Answers

Analysis

Quick quiz

1 A new hotel construction project in Shenzen, mainland China
2 Hong Kong
3 In less than two years
4 He says he'll dive into Hong Kong's Victoria Harbour

Paragraph 1: Idioms

In this context, 'the small pond' is Hong Kong and 'out of water' is mainland China.

Paragraph 2–4: Check the facts

According to the article, only sentence 1 is <u>definitely</u> true. These words and phrases indicate that the statements are not definitely true: looks like, industry insiders are saying, claimed, rumours.

Read his thoughts

There's no one correct answer to this question: it's simply to help the students focus on the problems that Alan Peng is facing.

Summary

The decisionmaker	Alan Peng
The decision	How should he respond to the newspaper article?
The issues	1 Is there really a problem here, or is it better if Peng ignores the article?
	2 If there is a problem, what exactly is it?
	3 What is the most appropriate action to take?

A possible solution

Alan Peng cannot allow these stories about his business to continue to circulate. In particular, he needs to do something about the rumours at the stock exchange, which could have a bad effect on his company's value and its ability to raise funds for new projects.

He is probably right to avoid taking direct action against the journalist or his newspaper, as a legal battle could do even more damage to his business. Instead, he should refute the claims made about his finances by publishing detailed information to show that his company's future is still strong.

The only way to counter the criticism made of his hotel project is to ensure that the hotel is completed as quickly as possible and to the highest standards. Should he honour his promise to jump into the harbour? Most people would understand that he made the promise as a joke – however, it would be a good publicity stunt!

The Barbecue

Before you read

This story is about a clash of cultures. If you want to find out more about cross-cultural issues, read this background box:

Background

> **Cross-cultural awareness**
>
> Culture plays a crucial part in shaping our values and the way we behave. To operate successfully in an international business environment, business-people have to understand the cultural differences between people from different backgrounds and nationalities. But how can they do this?
>
> Clearly, the average businessperson can't become an expert on all the world's cultures. So, management thinkers have suggested that instead of looking at cultures in detail, businesspeople should be aware of the differences between cultures, for example, by studying the ways cultures have different attitudes towards the individual, the environment or time.

One of the many areas of difference between cultures is in the attitude to privacy. Try this 'Way in' activity, to find out how different your attitudes are on this issue:

Way in

Which parts of your life do you consider public and which parts do you consider to be private?

First, draw two circles, one inside the other. The inner circle represents your private life, the outer your public life. The size of the circles should reflect how much of your life you think is public and how much is private.

Now put these things into the circle (private or public) in which you think they belong:

your living room   ,your car   your bathroom

your bedroom   your fridge

Compare your circles with a partner.

Now discuss this point:
Do you think that your choices are based more on cultural attitudes or on personal preferences?

Decisionmaker
The Barbecue

© Cambridge University Press 1997

The Barbecue

Problem

Wherever they were in the world, Koji Fukuhara and his British wife Judith always gave a summer barbecue party. Koji's job – working for a multinational company – meant that they had never stayed in one country for long, so the barbecue had always been an excellent way for them to mix socially with Koji's colleagues.

Now that Koji was in his first year as managing director of the company's Spanish subsidiary, the barbecue party had taken on an extra meaning. Managing people from twelve different nationalities was no easy task, but he was sure that the party would bring his whole team together. At least, that's what he hoped.

Koji and Judith Fukuhara

request the pleasure of your company
at a barbecue lunch

on Sunday 3 June, at 1.00
at Calle Gardenia 7, Sevilla

RSVP

Word file

multinational	a company which has offices or operations in many countries
to mix socially	to talk to lots of people in a friendly situation
subsidiary	a company which is more than 50% owned by the parent company
request the pleasure of your company	formal expression for 'invite you to'
RSVP	Répondez S'il Vous Plaît (French for 'please reply')

© Cambridge
University Press
1997

Here are two accounts of what happened at the party:

Etienne Briand (29 years old, French, in his second year as a middle manager in the Spanish office)

Alan McDyre (32 years old, American, a middle manager who has recently been transferred from the Los Angeles office)

'That new American guy is unbelievable! He arrived at Mr and Mrs Fukuhara's party an hour late — wearing a pair of bright green shorts, a running vest and a baseball cap! Can you imagine it? As far as I'm concerned, he made all of us managers look ridiculous. You could tell that the secretaries and the junior staff were laughing at him behind his back. I don't know how he expects us to command their respect, if he behaves so stupidly. Unfortunately, that wasn't the end of it. At about 2.45, Mr Fukuhara was standing by his pool, discussing one of the new projects with a few of us, when Alan came over and said, "Can I get anyone a drink from the fridge?"

It was extraordinary! Can you imagine offering people something from someone else's fridge — particularly when that person is your boss!

Well, we all just stopped talking and waited to see how Mr Fukuhara was going to handle the situation...'

'When I got there, the party was in full swing. Koji and Judith had invited everyone from the office, which meant I got the chance to meet all the people that I wouldn't normally speak to — you know, like the admin staff and the secretaries, even the cleaner! Of course, I realised immediately that I wasn't dressed quite right — the other guys were all in ties and blazers — but it was a Sunday and I thought, "Hey — they'll just have to take me as I am." Anyway, after a while I walked over to join Koji and a group of managers who were chatting by the pool. I noticed that they didn't have any drinks, so I said, "Can I get anyone a drink from the fridge?"

It was weird. For some reason, they all stopped talking and stared at me — like I'd committed some awful crime. Well, I didn't think I'd done anything wrong, so I just looked at Koji and waited for him to say something...'

Free discussion

If you were in Koji Fukuhara's situation, how would you respond to Alan's offer?

Word file

middle manager	one of a group of managers below top management
in full swing	full of people, with lots of activity
admin	abbreviation for 'administration'
blazer	a type of semi-smart jacket, usually with metal buttons
take me as I am	accept me as I am
a running vest	a shirt without sleeves, worn by athletes
behind his back	without his knowledge
to command respect	to get respect

Photocopiable

Decisionmaker
The Barbecue

© Cambridge University Press
1997

Analysis

What's it for?
Read the first two paragraphs and then choose the best answer to this question:
What's the purpose of this barbecue party?
a) To celebrate Koji Fukuhara's new job.
b) To improve his career prospects.
c) To mix socially with his colleagues.
d) To bring his team together.
e) To maintain a tradition.

The invitation
Look at the invitation and discuss these questions:
1 Do you need to reply formally to the invitation?
2 Should you take anything to the party?
3 How would you dress for a party like this?
4 What time would you arrive?

The two accounts: what's wrong?
Read the two accounts of the party and then try this activity:
Do you think that Alan has done anything wrong? If your answer is 'No', relax! If your answer is 'Yes', make a list of the things that you think he has done wrong and compare your list with the lists of your colleagues.

The two accounts: a cross-cultural reading
Here are four ways in which cultures may differ from each other. In small groups, discuss each of these points, with reference to Alan and Etienne, producing evidence to support your answers:

1 Specific v Diffuse
'Specific' cultures make a very clear distinction between working life and personal life; in 'diffuse' cultures these two areas of life are mixed up.
Which character takes a more 'diffuse' view of life?

2 The individual v The group
In some cultures, the interests of the group are more important than the interests of the individual; other cultures place far more emphasis on individual rights and responsibilities.
Which character is more individualistic?

3 Power distance
Cultures with a 'high power distance' place a great deal of importance on rank and status in organisations. Relationships in cultures with a 'low power distance' are much more equal.
Which character seems to come from a 'high power distance' culture?

4 Private and public space
Different cultures have different attitudes towards privacy.
Who shows more respect for private space?

Decisionmaker
The Barbecue

© Cambridge
University Press
1997

A conclusion?

Does this cross-cultural reading help to explain Alan's behaviour and Etienne's response to it?

Is culture relevant?

Now discuss these points:

1 Would Alan's behaviour be normal in an American context?
2 Is Etienne right to disapprove of Alan's behaviour?
3 Do you think that individual personality is more important than national culture in determining how Alan and Etienne behave at the barbecue?

When you've analysed both sides of the story, move on to the 'Decision time' section and decide what sort of action Koji Fukuhara should take.

Decisionmaker
The Barbecue

© Cambridge
University Press
1997

The decision

Decision time

How should Koji Fukuhara respond to Alan McDyre's behaviour?

Note: As a Japanese, Koji Fukuhara must have his own cultural perspective on the events at the barbecue. However, as a manager in a multi-cultural environment, he should be aware of the cultural backgrounds of his staff and be able to reach a fair, balanced decision.

What he could say...

Here are four things that he could say to Alan:

1 Thanks Alan, that would be great. Another drink for everyone.

2 Come with me. I think we should have a word in private.

3 How dare you! You should know your place.

4 Thank you for offering, Alan, but I think I'll get the drinks.

Discuss these two questions:
1 Which response would Alan expect?
2 Which response would Etienne want Koji to make?

What should he say?

Now decide!

What course of action should Koji Fukuhara take?

Decisionmaker
The Barbecue

© Cambridge
University Press
1997

At a glance

Topic:	Cross-cultural awareness
New vocabulary:	Socialising
Scenario:	A Japanese managing director has to decide whether a young American manager is behaving badly at a social event.

Answers

Analysis

What's it for?

d)

The invitation

Answers to these questions will vary enormously from culture to culture. However, here are a few suggestions:

1 Yes – that's what RSVP asks you to do
2 The answers to this question will be <u>very</u> different in different cultures, but most businesspeople working for multinationals would probably not expect a gift.
3 A barbecue is normally an informal event, but the invitation is fairly formal – and it's from the boss! Normal business clothes would not be suitable, but it's probably best to look reasonably smart.
4 Another tricky question to answer but probably any time between 1.05 and 1.20 would be suitable.

The two accounts: What's wrong?

Many people will say that Alan's done nothing wrong. However, here are three possibilities that some might suggest:

He arrived late

He was inappropriately dressed

He offered guests drinks from Koji's fridge

Decision time

What he could say...

1 a)
2 c)

Summary

The decisionmaker	Koji Fukuhara
The decision	How should he respond to Alan McDyre's behaviour?
The issues	1 Is Alan behaving badly?
	2 Are Alan's behaviour and Etienne's response to it products of their cultures?
	3 Does Koji need to take any action? If so, what should he do?

A possible solution

Although Alan's behaviour is nothing like as bad as Etienne suggests, Koji should take some action. Alan's behaviour may well be acceptable in an American context, but he has been arrogant in assuming that people will 'take him as he is' wherever he goes. As this is a new posting for him, and in a new country, he should have taken advice from more experienced colleagues on how to dress, behave, etc. before going to his boss's barbecue. Koji's best course of action is probably to let Alan get the drinks without further comment, but to have a quiet word with him at the office later in the week, to point out that he should be more sensitive to other people's expectations in future.

Plague and Prejudice

Before you read

This story concerns an outbreak of the disease known as 'the plague'. Read this background box to find out more about this disease:

Background

The plague

For most of human history, the plague has been one of the most feared diseases in the world. It is estimated that the European plague of the fourteenth century may have killed up to half of the population of Europe.

Modern medicine has brought the plague under control and it now occurs only in very dirty, unhealthy conditions. The outbreaks of plague in the Indian states of Gujarat and Maharasthra in 1994 were the first cases of the disease in India since 1966. However, the news of the plague caused widespread panic both in India and in the international community.

Way in

The behaviour of the American company in this story shows how fear and ignorance can influence decision-making. But, would your lack of knowledge of certain situations also make you jump to the wrong conclusions? Try this 'Way in' activity:

Discuss these two questions:

1 Your government wants to spend a large sum of money on improving public safety. It can invest in new safety equipment at the main airport or it can contribute to an international project to prevent asteroids (rocky objects in space) from hitting the earth. Which project would you vote for?

2 Is it more dangerous to be a member of the US armed forces in a time of war or to live in the American capital, Washington DC?

Now, see if the statistics your teacher has could change your point of view. Then discuss this point:

Do you think the statistics give a fair picture of the dangers of the four situations?

Decisionmaker
Plague and Prejudice

© Cambridge University Press 1997

Plague and Prejudice

Problem

Javesh Chandrasekar couldn't concentrate on the international radio news as he drove to his office in the southern Indian city of Bangalore. The following day he was leaving for a conference in Hawaii, organised by his company's biggest customer, and his mind was on all the things that he still had to organise. But as he drove into the company car park, an item on the news programme caught his attention.

'In the state of Maharasthra in central India, over a thousand cases of plague have now been reported. World Health Organisation officials have appealed for calm, as tens of thousands of villagers in the area flee their homes. Indian authorities say that it is too early to talk of an epidemic, but a number of Western travel agents are advising customers to travel to the region only if strictly necessary…'

Javesh switched off the radio irritably, grabbed his case and slammed his car door. Why did the international media always portray his country in such a negative light? Like any huge nation, India had its bad points – he accepted that – but, as he pointed out to visitors to his own company, in some fields India was a match for any country in the world.

He and his partner, Shiva Ramanajun, owned a software development company that produced new software for some of America's top corporations. A satellite link kept them in constant contact with their customers, they employed the cream of India's computer technicians but, thanks to low local labour costs, they could do the work for a fraction of the price demanded by a similar organisation in the West.

Word file

Bangalore	India's main centre for hi-tech industries
plague	a deadly disease, usually transmitted from rats to humans
to flee	to escape from
epidemic	a disease which affects a large number of people at the same time and spreads very quickly
to slam	to close violently
media	newspapers, television and radio
in a negative light	in a way that shows the bad side
to be a match	to be a serious competitor
software development	the writing of programs which tell a computer how to operate
satellite link	a telecommunications connection made through a satellite above the earth's atmosphere
the cream	the best

Decisiomaker
Plague and Prejudice

© Cambridge University Press 1997

Still fuming about the radio report, Javesh strode into his office, where he found Shiva in a state of considerable agitation. 'What is it?' he asked. Shiva didn't say anything, but handed him a page of fax paper.

Page 2 of 2

Dear Javesh:
We've heard the bad news coming out of India over the last couple of days, and let me say that we're real sorry to hear about the plague problems that you're experiencing.
Our travel people tell me that they're expecting a lot of flight cancellations into and out of India over the next few days and we quite understand that it may now be difficult for you to attend our Hawaii conference as planned.
Of course, as one of our most valued suppliers, we want to make sure that you don't miss the party, so we'll be arranging a satellite hook-up from the Hawaii centre to enable you to video-conference with us throughout the whole three days.
All cancellation arrangements and expenses will be handled by our travel people here, so there's nothing for you to worry about on that score.
With best wishes

Miriam T Yersinia

Hawaii Conference Co-ordinator

Javesh couldn't contain his anger. 'Are these people mad?' he shouted. 'Why are they trying to stop me going to their conference? Do they understand nothing about our country? What do they think I'm going to do? Give them the plague? Maharasthra's over a thousand kilometres away. I ask you, Shiva, I ask you – how can we do business with people like this?'

'Javesh, calm down,' said Shiva, 'and think carefully before you do anything. We both know that there are no flight cancellations out of Bangalore and we both know that these people are being very very stupid – but they are also our biggest customer.'

Free discussion

How should Javesh respond to the fax?

Word file

to fume	to be very angry about something
in a state of agitation	in an emotional or anxious condition
a hook up	a connection
to video-conference	to take part in a conference where participants are in different places and communicate via a video screen
on that score	concerning that matter

Decisionmaker
Plague and Prejudice

© Cambridge University Press 1997

Analysis

Paragraph 1: Set the scene
Read the opening paragraph and answer these questions:
1 Where does Javesh work?   3 What's the purpose of his trip?
2 Where's he going tomorrow?

Paragraph 2: The radio report
International news stories are usually put together from a number of different sources.
Here are three of the statements on which the radio report is based. Write
the source of each statement in the column on the right.

	Statement	Source
1	We ask you to be calm.	
2	It is too early to talk of an epidemic.	
3	You should only travel to this region if strictly necessary.	

Paragraph 3: Javesh's reaction
Read the paragraph and then discuss these points:
1 India has a population of around 900 million. In this context, should the
   deaths of 1000 people from plague have such extensive media coverage?
2 Do you understand why Javesh is so angry about the media coverage?

Paragraph 4: The software development company
Read the paragraph and complete this company profile:

> **Bangalore Software Development**
>
> Owners: ....
>
> Main customers: ....
>
> How is the company connected to its main markets? ....
>
> What kind of people does it employ? ....
>
> Are its services cheaper or more expensive than similar services in the West? ....

The fax
Read the fax and answer these questions:
1 What is the sender of the fax sorry to hear about?
2 Why will it be difficult for Javesh to attend the conference?
3 What special arrangements will be made for him?

Now discuss these questions:
1 From what you heard in the radio report, do you think that flights into and
   out of India will be cancelled?
2 Does it sound as if the Americans really want Javesh to attend the
   conference? Why not?

Read to the end of the story and then move on to discuss your decision.

Decisiomaker
**Plague and
Prejudice**

© Cambridge
University Press
1997

The decision

Decision time

How should Javesh respond to the fax?

It is probably quite clear what Javesh would like to say in response to this fax. But, as Shiva says, before he takes his decision, he needs to think carefully. To think about the diplomatic implications of any decision that he might take, try this activity:

Being diplomatic

When you're being diplomatic, what you really want to say and what you actually say can be very different. Look again at the fax from Miriam T Yersinia. Around it are the four things that she probably really wanted to say. Draw a line from each statement to the paragraph of the fax that you think expresses that statement 'diplomatically'.

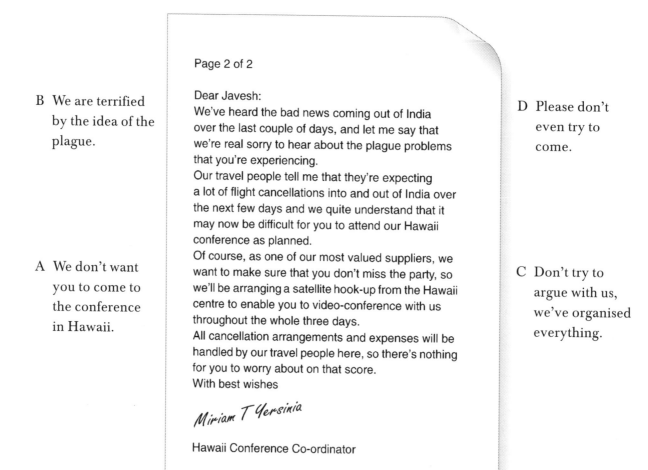

B We are terrified by the idea of the plague.

A We don't want you to come to the conference in Hawaii.

D Please don't even try to come.

C Don't try to argue with us, we've organised everything.

Page 2 of 2

Dear Javesh:
We've heard the bad news coming out of India over the last couple of days, and let me say that we're real sorry to hear about the plague problems that you're experiencing.
Our travel people tell me that they're expecting a lot of flight cancellations into and out of India over the next few days and we quite understand that it may now be difficult for you to attend our Hawaii conference as planned.
Of course, as one of our most valued suppliers, we want to make sure that you don't miss the party, so we'll be arranging a satellite hook-up from the Hawaii centre to enable you to video-conference with us throughout the whole three days.
All cancellation arrangements and expenses will be handled by our travel people here, so there's nothing for you to worry about on that score.
With best wishes

Miriam T Yersinia

Hawaii Conference Co-ordinator

Decisionmaker
Plague and Prejudice

© Cambridge University Press 1997

Here are four things that Javesh would probably like to say in response to the fax. In pairs, discuss how he could put each of these ideas across diplomatically:

What he would like to say...	What he should say...
1 Why are you trying to stop me going to your conference?	
2 You are lying to me: there are no flight cancellations out of Bangalore.	
3 You know nothing at all about the situation in my country.	
4 How can I do business with stupid, ignorant people like you?	

Now, with someone from a different pair, role play a conversation between Miriam and Javesh in which each of you tries to put your points across as diplomatically as possible.

The options

Having thought through how Javesh can put his points across diplomatically, think about the two decisions that he has to take:

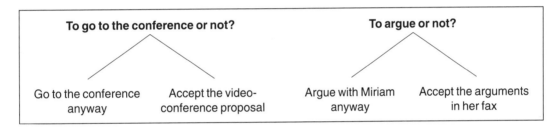

To go to the conference or not?

Go to the conference anyway   Accept the video-conference proposal

To argue or not?

Argue with Miriam anyway   Accept the arguments in her fax

Now decide!

In your pairs, discuss the implications of each possible decision and then choose one of the options for each of the two decisions. (NB: You need to make two decisions to solve this problem.)
Of course, you may be able to think of a much better solution – in which case, go for it!

Decisiomaker
Plague and Prejudice

© Cambridge University Press 1997

At a glance

Topic:	Software development, disease, prejudices
New vocabulary:	High technology
Scenario:	An outbreak of plague threatens to stop the owner of an Indian software company attending an international conference.

Answers

Way in

These statistics may surprise your students:

1 Statisticians say that you are over three times more likely to die as the result of an asteroid strike than in a plane crash. The chances of an asteroid killing you are approximately 1 in 6,000; your chances of dying in a plane crash are 1 in 20,000.

2 The USA sent 420,000 service people to the 1991 Gulf war. Of these, 148 died in action – a rate of approximately 35 per 100,000. By contrast the murder rate in Washington DC in 1992 was 75 per 100,000.

Analysis

Paragraph 1: Set the scene

1 Bangalore in southern India
2 Hawaii
3 To attend a conference organised by his biggest customer.

Paragraph 2: The radio report

1 The World Health Organisation
2 Indian authorities
3 Western travel agents

Paragraph 4: The software development company

Owners: Javesh Chandrasekar and Shiva Ramanajun

Main customers: Top American corporations

How is the company connected to its main markets?: By satellite link

What kind of people does it employ?: The cream of India's computer technicians

Are its services cheaper or more expensive than similar services in the West?: Much cheaper

The fax

1 She's sorry to hear about the outbreak of plague in India.
2 Because of the cancellation of flights into and out of India.
3 They'll arrange a satellite link to Hawaii, so that Javesh can participate in the conference by video.

Decision time

Being diplomatic
para 1: b)   para 2: a)
para 3: d)   para 4: c)

Summary

The decisionmaker	Javesh Chandrasekar
The decision	How should Javesh respond to the fax from his American customer?
The issues	1 Should Javesh go to the conference, or should he accept their offer to use video conferencing facilities?
	2 Should he explain to the Americans why their assumptions about the plague in India are so wrong?
	3 What are the implications for their long-term business relationship?

A possible solution

There are no practical reasons to stop Javesh from attending the conference and so, obviously, he should go. He is justifiably angry about the ignorance shown by his American partners and he should make this clear to them. Of course, there is no point in offending his biggest customer, but, while being diplomatic, it is important for their long-term relationship that Javesh makes his point as strongly as possible.

Follow-up activity

Write a fax for Javesh to send to the American company, explaining what he intends to do and why.

The Abalone Mystery

Before you read

This story is about the abalone fishing industry. To find out more about the abalone business, read this background box:

Background

> **Abalone**
>
> Abalone is a type of edible shellfish found in the sea off southern Australia, New Zealand and South Africa. Because stocks are limited, strict laws govern the amount of abalone that can be caught and the divers who collect abalone must be licensed. But, as a result of the huge demand for abalone in the markets of China and south east Asia, illegal abalone fishing is common and in Australia it is regarded as a type of organised crime by the authorities.

This story asks you to do some detective work. But what kind of detective would you be? Just for fun, try this detective's aptitude test.

Way in

Choose one answer to each of these questions

1 A car alarm goes off in your street at two o'clock in the morning. What do you do?
  a) Go back to sleep.
  b) Go out in the street to investigate.
  c) Call the police.

2 You arrive home to find a message on your answerphone that says, 'You are going to die!' How do you react?
  a) Ignore it.
  b) Check all the doors are locked and sleep with a knife next to your bed.
  c) Call the police.

3 A man stops you in a dark street and demands your money. Do you:
  a) Hand it over?
  b) Fight?
  c) Scream and run away?

Now work out your score. Score 5 points for every answer (a), 3 points for every answer (b) and 1 point for every answer (c). Then add up your scores and see how you do on the *Decisionmaker* assessment.

15 points	You'd make a good detective: you have a cool, practical response to a crisis.
10–14	You're a tough, decisive character, but you may have a tendency to look for the worst in situations.
6–9	When analysing a case, think carefully before you jump to any conclusions.
less than 5	You rely too much on the help and opinions of others: you should have more faith in your own judgement.

Decisionmaker
The Abalone Mystery

© Cambridge University Press 1997

The Abalone Mystery

Problem

When the body of South Australian businessman, Ron Massie was found washed up on a beach early in the morning of 1 April 1996, the local police were inclined to treat it as a tragic accident. But detective Jane Murphy wasn't so sure – particularly when she started examining some of the key documents in the case.

THE SOUTHERN STAR 16.2.95

MR NICE GUY TAKES THE PLUNGE

by Rita Napangadi

Ron Massie

Adelaide businessman, Ron Massie, today announced a bold new business venture – a new abalone-canning plant on the western fringes of the city. Ron, who is also well-known for his charity work, knows that this is one project in which he can't afford to give anything away.

'Efficiency and strict cost control are the keys to success in this business', he says. 'We know that for every A$1 million of cans that we ship, we'll have spent A$800,000 on the raw material alone. That means that we've got very little margin for error.'

The waters off South Australia are one of the few places where abalone still thrive, but, even so, supplies are strictly limited – a problem that Ron says he can deal with: 'Using the most advanced canning technology in the world means that we can extract the maximum amount of abalone meat from each catch. No waste! No worries!'

17.2.95

Dear Mr Massie

As you know, to protect the abalone stocks in Australian waters, abalone fishing is subject to a strict quota system and all abalone divers must be licensed.

If you have any doubts about the source of any abalone that you are offered, please don't hesitate to get in touch with us.

I look forward to working closely with you.

Yours sincerely

1.00 a.m. 9/6/95

Ron – I know this is a bad start to your day, but we're experiencing a persistent malfunction with the sealing procedure on the canning line. I've been up half the night with a couple of blokes trying to fix it, but so far, no joy. Without a miracle first thing this morning, I reckon we're set to lose about 40% of the latest abalone delivery.

Pete

Word file

washed up	left by the sea
Mr Nice Guy	someone whom everyone likes
to take the plunge	to start a risky activity
to thrive	to be successful and strong
catch	a delivery of fish
no worries	Australian slang for 'no problem'
a quota	a fixed amount
malfunction	a fault in an operation
sealing	the process of closing cans to keep air out
canning line	a production line where a product is put into cans
blokes	men (slang)
no joy	no success

Decisionmaker
The Abalone Mystery

© Cambridge University Press 1997

14/8/95

Dear Ron,

I've looked over the figures and, frankly, they scare me. As you said, there's no margin for error in this business and at the moment your company is making far too many big, big errors.

Unless you can do something drastic – like reducing your overheads or slashing your raw material costs – I just don't see how you can go on.

My advice is – cut your losses and get out now.

Gina

23/8/95

YES. CAN DO. I'VE TALKED TO MY PARTNERS AND WE CAN OFFER YOU WHAT YOU WANT AT THE PRICE WE TALKED ABOUT. CASH ON DELIVERY. NO WORRIES.

RP

THE SOUTHERN STAR 29.1.96

CAPTAIN RON SERVES UP A CHINESE SURPRISE

by Rita Napangadi

Adelaide businessman Ron Massie celebrated a remarkable first year at the helm of his new company with the purchase of a company yacht, the *Mother of Pearl*.

Although he refused to go into details, results for his abalone-canning business look set to defy all expectations. Asked about the reasons for his spectacular success, a grinning Ron gave a one word answer: 'China'.

He went on to explain, 'In China, no wedding feast or festival is complete without abalone on the menu. And,

Ron Massie's new yacht, the Mother of Pearl.

with the Chinese economy booming, we just haven't been able to ship the abalone fast enough!'.

5/2/96

Dear Ron,

I enjoyed your publicity stunt with the yacht last week – but, believe me, you haven't fooled anybody. Half of Adelaide knows what's really going on, and that includes your creditors.

As for the accounts – when the tax people get to grips with all these mysterious payments, they're going to throw a real wobbly!

We <u>have</u> to talk!

Gina

Word file

to slash	to reduce dramatically
to cut your losses	to withdraw from an unprofitable business before you lose any more money
at the helm	to be in charge of a boat or a business
to defy expectations	to perform in an unexpected way
a publicity stunt	a special event designed to get lots of publicity
to fool someone	to deceive someone
to get to grips with	to deal seriously with
to throw a wobbly	to become very angry and upset

Photocopiab

Decisionmaker
The Abalone Mystery

© Cambridge University Press 1997

14/2/96

YOU STILL OWE US. NEXT MONTH WE CUT YOUR SUPPLIES. THE MONTH AFTER WE'LL CUT SOMETHING ELSE UNDERSTAND?

RP

Dear Ron,   19/2/96

Sorry to see you looking so down on Saturday night, mate. Still, at least it looks like there's light at the end of the tunnel.

If you ever fancy a few days away from it all in the country, give us a call – Sheila and I would be delighted to have you.

Give us a call soon about that fishing trip we discussed.

All the best,   Bruce

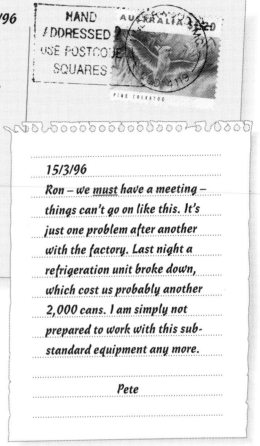

HAND ADDRESSED
USE POSTCODE SQUARES
PINK COCKATOO

15/3/96

Ron – we *must* have a meeting – things can't go on like this. It's just one problem after another with the factory. Last night a refrigeration unit broke down, which cost us probably another 2,000 cans. I am simply not prepared to work with this sub-standard equipment any more.

Pete

THE SOUTHERN STAR 2.4.96

BUSINESSMAN'S DEATH A TRAGIC LESSON

by Rita Napangadi

Tributes to the Adelaide businessman, Ron Massie, continue to pour in. Massie, whose body was found washed up on the beach yesterday, was the boss of SA Abalone and was well-known for his charity work.

But local lifeguards were quick to draw a lesson from his death. 'I guess he went for a swim and got swept away,' said their spokesperson, Rick Peebles. 'We're always warning about the strong currents that you get round here. After this perhaps a

Local businessman Ron Massie, whose body was found yesterday

few more people will start listening.'

If you were detective Jane Murphy, how would you explain the death of Ron Massie to your superior officer?

Free discussion

abc

Word file

to look 'down'	to appear unhappy or depressed
mate	slang for friend
light at the end of the tunnel	a possible end to your problems
refrigeration unit	equipment used to keep something cool
a lifeguard	a person employed on a beach to help swimmers who are in danger
a tribute	a message of respect and admiration
currents	areas of water which flow strongly

Decisionmaker
The Abalone Mystery

© Cambridge University Press 1997

Analysis

Read through the documents and then work in small groups, discussing the answers to the following:

The characters

Make sure that you are clear about the roles the different characters play in the story. Match the job in the column on the left with a name from the column on the right.

Job	Character
the detective	Bruce
the boss	Rita Napangadi
the factory manager	Ron Massie
the accountant	Pete
the journalist	Gina
the friend	Jane Murphy

Do you have any theories about what job the mysterious 'RP' does?

The abalone business

Complete this sentence by choosing two factors from the box below:

Success in the abalone business depends on:

> good labour relations   strong cash flow   efficiency
> strict cost control   new ideas   aggressive marketing

The legal situation

Which of these statements best describes the legal position of abalone fishing in Australia?

1 There are no regulations concerning abalone fishing.
2 People can collect as much abalone as they like, but they must have a licence to do so.
3 The amount of abalone collected is subject to a quota and all abalone divers must be licensed.
4 Everyone has a right to collect a small amount of abalone.

The accounts

What can you deduce about the financial position of Ron Massie's company at two points in its history: after six months, and after a year?

After six months...

1 Did the financial position of the company look good?
2 Had any mistakes been made?
3 Were there any ways in which the company could improve its performance?

After a year...

4 Did the business owe anyone any money?
5 Were all payments made by the business clearly explained?
6 Were there likely to be any problems with the tax people?

Decisionmaker
The Abalone Mystery

© Cambridge University Press 1997

Production problems

Complete these two entries in the factory manager's records:

Date	Technical problem	Result
		Loss of 40% of abalone delivery Loss of 2,000 çans

Now discuss this:

Do you have the impression that these were the only two production problems that Pete had to deal with?

Public image

Choose two adjectives which describe the public image of Ron Massie:

ruthless   generous   popular   tough

mean   aggressive   corrupt   weak

Next, discuss the public image of his company:

1 Are you surprised that Ron Massie's company can afford a company yacht?
2 What reason does Ron Massie give for his company's success?
3 Do you think that everyone believes that the company is so successful?

Now discuss this point:

Do you think that there's a difference between the reality and the public image of Ron Massie and his company?

The 'RP' letters

Do you have any theories about the 'RP' letters? Discuss these three questions:

1 In the 23/8/95 letter, what does 'we can offer you what you want' refer to?
2 What are the 'supplies' mentioned in the 14/2/96 letter?
3 What is the meaning of 'we'll cut something else'?

Unfinished business?

Discuss which of these things on Ron's 'To Do' list had probably not been dealt with at the time of his death.

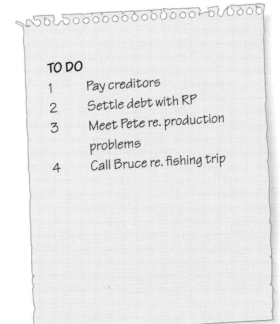

TO DO
1   Pay creditors
2   Settle debt with RP
3   Meet Pete re. production problems
4   Call Bruce re. fishing trip

Decisionmaker
The Abalone Mystery

© Cambridge University Press 1997

The decision

Decision time

How would you explain the death of Ron Massie?

Prepare the case

Divide into three groups. Each group should work on one of the following three tasks:

1 Suicide

Try to build a case to persuade the rest of the class that Ron Massie's death was suicide.

2 Murder

Work on a way of telling the story that will persuade the others that Ron's death was murder. You'll need to find a convincing motive – and a possible murderer.

3 Accident

Look for arguments that suggest that Ron's death was an accident, as well as ways of undermining possible arguments in favour of suicide and murder.

Present the case

Each group should elect a spokesperson to put their case to the rest of the class. The spokesperson should present the case formally and allow time at the end of the presentation for group colleagues to make any extra points in support of that argument.

Jury discussion

Form another three groups, each one containing roughly equal numbers of representatives from the original three groups. These three new groups should discuss the case, take a vote on their decision and then present their findings to the class as a whole.

Finally, the class can vote on which alternative is the most convincing.

Photocopiable

Decisionmaker
**The Abalone
Mystery**

© Cambridge
University Press
1997

At a glance

Topic:	Solving a mystery in the food processing industry
New vocabulary:	The food and fishing industries, production, colloquial expressions
Scenario:	The body of an Australian businessman is found on a beach. Was it an accident, suicide or murder?

Answers

Analysis

The characters
the detective: Jane Murphy
the boss: Ron Massie
the factory manager: Pete
the accountant: Gina
the journalist: Rita Napangadi
the friend: Bruce

The abalone business
strict cost control and efficiency

The legal situation: 3

The accounts
1 No (the figures 'scare' the accountant – 14/8/95)
2 Yes ('big, big errors' – 14/8/95)
3 Yes (Gina says 'reduce your overheads, slash your raw material costs'… or 'get out now' – 14/8/95)
4 Yes (see reference to 'creditors' – 5/2/96)
5 No (see reference to 'mysterious payments' – 5/2/96)
6 Yes (the tax people will 'throw a real wobbly' – 5/2/96)

Public image
Ron Massie (*suggested answers*) popular, generous

The company's image:
1 You probably should be surprised by the purchase of the company yacht – the letter from Gina suggested that the company was losing money
2 The booming Chinese market
3 No – Gina's letter of 5/2/96 suggests that Ron hasn't 'fooled anybody'.

The 'RP' letters (suggested answers)
1 Abalone
2 Abalone
3 It's up to your imagination!

Unfinished business
Judging by the documents on Jane's desk, it's probable that none of these things had been dealt with at the time of Ron's death.

Production problems

Date	Technical problem	Result
10/6/95	Persistent malfunction with the sealing procedure	Loss of 40% of abalone delivery
15/3/96	Break down of refrigeration unit	Loss of 2,000 cans

Discussion: No. Pete says 'It's just one problem after another'.

Summary

The decisionmaker	Jane Murphy
The decision	How should she explain Ron Massie's death to her superior officer?
The issues	1 Does the evidence point to a suicide?
	2 Is there a suspicion that Massie was murdered?
	3 Or does the evidence suggest that it was an accident?

A possible solution

There is no one clear solution to this problem: you should be able to make a fairly convincing case for each of the three options suggested.

Follow-up activity

Imagine that you are going to make *The Abalone Mystery* into a Hollywood movie. Write a short summary of the story and choose the actors and actresses that you'd like to see playing the parts.

The Hohokum Virus

Before you read

In 'The Hohokum Virus' you'll read about computer crime and computer viruses. If you want to find out more about these viruses, read this background box:

Background

> ### Computer viruses
>
> Computer viruses are the biggest threat to modern computer systems. Viruses are tiny programs which spread through computer networks destroying a computer's memory and deleting its programs and files. They are often introduced into computer software by criminals who hope to get money from a company. A recent survey suggested that computers in big firms suffer from an average of four viruses per year.

And if you'd like to think about some of the issues involved in computer crime, discuss the two cases in the 'Way in' section:

Way in

Computer crime is becoming increasingly common in the modern world. But is it really as bad as more traditional forms of crime? Compare these two cases:

The bank raid

A bank robber walks into a bank with a gun, threatens the bank clerk and steals $50,000.

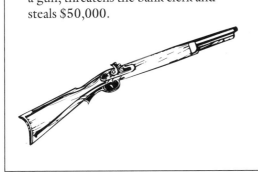

The salami attack

A computer expert gets into a bank's computer system, takes $0.01 from 5 million different accounts and transfers the money to his or her own account.

Which crime is worse?

Decisionmaker
The Hohokum Virus

© Cambridge University Press 1997

The Hohokum Virus

Problem

Hohokum Systems Inc. is an electronic data systems company founded in the mid-1980s by three young friends, Matt Bradley, Jane Goodall and Riccardo Ciccone. Based in Phoenix, Arizona, Hohokum specialises in providing secure computer systems for clients who are highly sensitive to the dangers of fraud and computer crime. Working mostly in the financial and local government sectors, Hohokum successfully came through the recession of the early 90's and is now well established across the Western USA. Recently it has expanded its sales operation to cover a number of countries in Central America.

But, despite such spectacular growth, Hohokum's management structure has changed little since the early days of the company. Decision-making over all issues relating to policy, day-to-day management and expenditure is still strictly controlled by the three partners. However, Hohokum's staff are happy – the Phoenix office is relaxed and easy-going and a profit share scheme ensures that all employees identify strongly with Hohokum's corporate objectives.

So, when Bradley, Goodall and Ciccone flew to Mexico City to attempt to clinch the company's biggest ever deal, they knew that the staff back in Phoenix were 100% behind them. They had an afternoon meeting with the top officials of the Mexican state post and telecommunications company. It was the culmination of two years' sustained sales pressure and, if successful, the deal to set up an EDS for the Mexican government could be worth as much as $35 million.

Word file

EDS (electronic data systems)	computer systems
fraud	the crime of deceiving people to obtain money, or goods
spectacular growth	great and rapid growth
profit share scheme	a plan that gives some of the company's profits to its staff
corporate objectives	the targets set by a company
to clinch a deal	to make a sale
culmination	the result of a lot of effort and hard work

Decisionmaker
The Hohokum Virus

© Cambridge University Press 1997

The three partners had taken a 09.30 flight out of Phoenix and were due to arrive in Mexico City in good time for lunch with their Mexican agent. Back in Hohokum's office, the atmosphere was tense as Hohokum's staff drank coffee and discussed the company's chances of success. But at around 10.00 that morning, the tension turned to panic when the following message flashed up on every work station computer terminal in the Hohokum building:

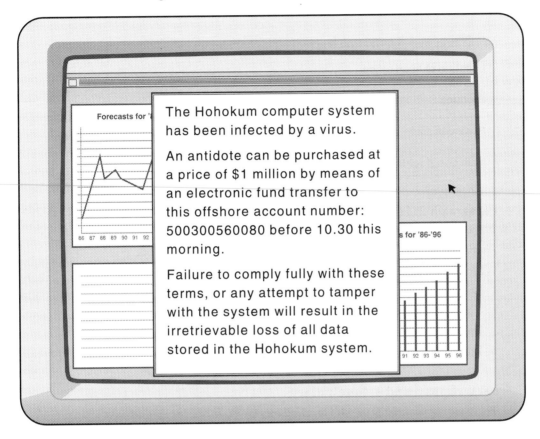

> Forecasts for '
>
> The Hohokum computer system has been infected by a virus.
>
> An antidote can be purchased at a price of $1 million by means of an electronic fund transfer to this offshore account number: 500300560080 before 10.30 this morning.
>
> Failure to comply fully with these terms, or any attempt to tamper with the system will result in the irretrievable loss of all data stored in the Hohokum system.

The staff stared at their screens in amazement. They knew that their three bosses were all in the air and couldn't be contacted. 'Is this some kind of joke?' they asked each other.

Free discussion

Should Hohokum's staff pay the ransom?

Word file

antidote	a program that will stop the virus
electronic fund transfer	the direct payment of money from one account to another by computer
offshore account	a bank account in a country like the Bahamas or the Cayman Islands with special banking laws. Accounts in these places are often secret.
to tamper	to interfere or to make changes

Analysis

Read through 'The Hohokum Virus', stopping at the end of each paragraph to answer or discuss these questions:

Paragraph 1: Company profile

Complete this company profile sheet with information about Hohokum Systems from the first paragraph:

Name:
Location of head office:
Product:
Business areas of main clients:
Main geographical areas of operation:

Paragraph 2: Hohokum's employees

When you've read the second paragraph, think about conditions for Hohokum's employees:

Which of these sentences are true and which are false?

1 Employees often take important decisions.
2 There is a pressurised, competitive atmosphere at the company.
3 Employees have a chance to share in the company's profits.
4 Employees have no interest in company policy.

Paragraphs 3 and 4: Jane's diary

When you've read the third and fourth paragraphs, fill in the gaps in Jane Goodall's diary:

Tuesday July 6

AM

09.30 Fly to ¹ ....

Lunch with ² ....

....

PM

Meeting with ³ ....

to discuss ⁴ ....

Wednesday July 7

AM

PM

The message

Read to the end of the text, look at the message on the computer screen and answer these questions:

1 How can the virus be stopped?
2 Why do you think that Hohokum is asked to use electronic fund transfer?
3 Why does the person want the money to go to an offshore account?
4 What is worrying about the time?
5 What will happen if Hohokum doesn't pay?
6 What will happen if someone interferes with the computer system?

Now move on to make your decision.

The decision

Decision time

Should the staff pay the ransom?

Try thinking about the problem in this way:

The decision tree

The decision tree is a method used by many businesspeople to think about the alternatives in a situation and their possible consequences. This decision tree shows the alternatives and their possible consequences in Hohokum's situation.

Work in pairs or in small groups and follow the steps along each branch of the tree. Decide on your answers to the four questions.

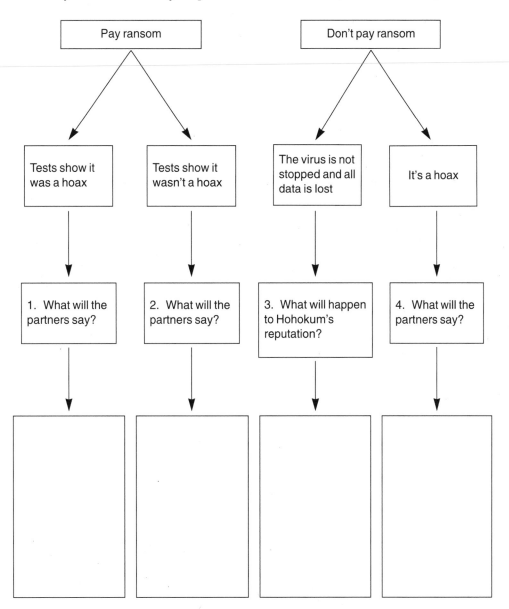

Now decide!

What should the staff do?

Decisionmaker
The Hohokum Virus

© Cambridge University Press 1997

At a glance

Topic:	Computer security and computer viruses
New vocabulary:	Computers
Scenario:	A computer systems company is blackmailed by someone who claims to have infected its system with a computer virus.

Answers

Way in

Note: A 'salami attack' is a type of computer fraud in which very small amounts are taken from a very large number of accounts.

Financially neither crime is worse than the other, as the same amount of money is stolen in both cases. However, you could say that the bank raid is worse because of the threat of the gun.

Analysis

Paragraph 1: Company profile

Name: Hohokum Systems
Head office: Phoenix, Arizona
Product: secure computer systems
Business areas of main clients:
finance, local government
Main geographical areas of operation:
Western USA, Central America

Paragraph 2: Hohokum's employees

1 false   2 false   3 true   4 false

Paragraphs 3 and 4: Jane's diary

1 Mexico City
2 Mexican agent
3 Mexican state post and telecommunications company
4 EDP system

The message

1 By buying an antidote.
2 Because it's a very quick, secret way of making a payment.
3 Because this account is in a different country and it only has a number, not a name.
4 It's 10.00 already, so the employees only have 30 minutes to make a decision.
5 All Hohokum's data will be lost.
6 All Hohokum's data will be lost.

Decision time

Decision tree

1 They'll probably be furious because such a lot of money was wasted.
2 They should be very relieved.
3 If anyone finds out what happened, it will be ruined.
4 They'll be very relieved.

Summary

The decisionmakers	Hohokum's staff
The decision	Should they pay the ransom demand?
The risks	1 If the ransom is not paid, the virus could badly damage Hohokum's computer system. 2 If the ransom is paid the threat could prove to be a hoax and Hohokum will have wasted a lot of money.
The issues	1 Do the staff have the right to take such an important decision in these circumstances? 2 Hohokum provides <u>secure</u> computer systems. How can its reputation be preserved?

Suggested activity: The crisis meeting

Set your class a 30-minute time limit in which to take the decision, and then get them to elect a chairperson who will be responsible for controlling the meeting and ensuring that a decision is taken within that time limit. After that, allow the chairperson to control things and just see what develops!

A possible solution

Hohokum's staff should decide to pay the ransom. If its customers find out that the company has been the victim of a virus, it will lose all credibility – and probably most of its business as well!

In the longer term, Hohokum should investigate how their security system was breached and improve it as soon as possible. Obviously, they should also try to find the criminal and recover the money – but only if they can do this without attracting publicity.

Wall Street Blues

Before you read

The story in this chapter is set in New York's financial centre, Wall Street. Two of the most important financial items bought and sold on Wall Street are stocks and bonds. When you buy stock in a company it means that you have bought a share in its ownership. When you own a company's bonds, it means that you have lent it money. To find out more about bonds, read this background box:

Background

> ### Bonds
>
> One of the ways in which big companies borrow money is to sell bonds. If you buy a bond from a company, you get a contract which tells you that the company will pay you a fixed rate of interest at regular intervals and that you'll be able to get your money back at a fixed date in the future – if the company still exists, of course (if the company goes bankrupt before this date, you normally get nothing!). But what happens if you want your money back before this fixed date? No problem – you simply sell the bond to someone else.
>
> But if you do this, you probably won't get the same price for the bond as you paid for it. The prices of bonds are always changing, for many reasons: for example, if people think that a company is going to go bankrupt, its bond prices will fall dramatically. This means that the bond market is a very risky place to invest money and the people who work there are normally under enormous pressure to take the right decisions.

Way in

People who work in financial markets like the bond market should try to assess the risks in these markets logically. But, most people agree that prices in these markets are really driven by two of the most basic human emotions – greed and fear.

1 So, how do **you** assess risk? Discuss these two alternatives:
   a) Would you prefer to have $85,000 or to have an 85% chance of winning $100,000?
   b) Would you prefer to lose $85,000 or to have an 85% chance of losing $100,000?
2 Discuss whether your choices are based on logic or emotion.

Decisionmaker
Wall Street Blues

© Cambridge University Press 1997

Wall Street Blues

The characters

Cliff Addis　*Bond salesperson, Hislop & Hislop Investment Bank*

'I sell millions of bonds every year to the top financial institutions in the USA. I have to persuade these people that the bonds I'm selling represent a great investment opportunity. So, a big part of my job is to find bonds that are going to increase in value. And how do I do that? Well, I say there's only one way to make real money in the bond markets – always do the unexpected!'

1

Arnie Arnopp　*Senior bond salesperson, Hislop & Hislop Investment Bank*

'You may think I'm old-fashioned, but I say the bond markets are a long-term bet. There are too many kids in the dealing room who don't think beyond tomorrow. They're always looking for a 'get rich quick' scheme. I tell my team that we need to build a relationship of trust with our customers.'

2

Louise Patterson　*Fund manager, Carte Pensions*

'In my job, I manage millions of dollars of other people's money. Ordinary working people pay into my pension fund; I invest their money in stocks, bonds or whatever I think is a good investment, and the money the fund generates pays these people's pensions when they retire.

This means I've got a huge responsibility: I can't afford to make mistakes with other people's money but, as a professional investor, I have to take risks to make sure I get the best deals possible.

3

The situation

Cliff Addis had never really known failure in his life. He'd gone straight from the top of his Harvard class to the dealing room of Hislop & Hislop, where he'd built a reputation as one of the best bond salespeople on Wall Street. But just lately, things hadn't been going so well for him. Only last week he'd persuaded his best customer, Louise Patterson of Carte Pensions, to buy $77 million worth of bonds in a New York property company: two days later the bonds had fallen in value by nearly 3%.

4

Word file

Wall Street	the New York street known as the financial centre of the USA
blues	a type of music in which people sing about being sad
investment bank	a bank that deals in buying and selling stocks and bonds
a long-term bet	a gamble that brings results after a long period of time
fund manager	a person who invests large amounts of individuals' or companies', money for them
pension fund	a quantity of money that is invested and used to pay people's retirement pensions
Harvard	one of the USA's top universities

Decisionmaker
Wall Street Blues

© Cambridge University Press 1997

He tried to re-assure her on the phone.

'Don't worry, Louise, it's a temporary situation. By the end of the month, those bonds will have turned round – I promise. And, anyway, I'm working on something right now that's going to be very special. Something totally new – you're going to love it!' 5

Cliff put down the phone and sat for a moment with his head in his hands. Everybody knew that the bonds in the property company weren't going to turn round – and he knew that he didn't have any good new investment ideas. 6

The idea

As his taxi took him home after work, Cliff scanned the evening's financial news in the newspaper. One headline caught his eye:

WISCONSIN CREDIT FACES BANKRUPTCY

THE WISCONSIN CREDIT BANK IS CLOSE TO BANKRUPTCY THIS EVENING AFTER A VOTE OF NO CONFIDENCE BY A NUMBER OF ITS KEY INVESTORS

7

His mind started racing. He knew that tomorrow there would be a mad rush to sell Wisconsin Credit bonds and the price would plunge. But would the bank really go bankrupt? Wisconsin Credit served a large number of Mid-West farming communities and Cliff knew that these people were a political priority for the government. If the bank went bankrupt, thousands of farmers would lose their life savings and the government would lose a lot of votes. The more he thought about it, the more certain he was the government would bail out the bank – and that meant that Wisconsin Credit bonds were a golden investment opportunity. 8

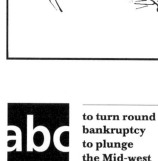

Word file

to turn round	to change direction
bankruptcy	the state of being unable to repay debts
to plunge	to fall dramatically
the Mid-west	the central and northern area of the USA
to bail out	to help a business in financial difficulty by giving it money

Decisionmaker
Wall Street Blues

© Cambridge University Pres 1997

He scribbled a few notes in his notebook:

Bonds in Wisconsin
Credit fall →
Buy them while they're
cheap →
Gov't bails out
Wisconsin Credit →
Bonds rise again →
sell = A KILLING!

9

The decision

Cliff had been in front of his computer terminal for nearly two hours by the time his boss, Arnie Arnopp, arrived for work at 8.30 the next day.

10

Arnie shouted across to Cliff as he walked in. 'What's your hot tip for today, Cliffy-boy? No, don't tell me. Let me guess. Wisconsin Credit! That would be just your style – bonds in a bankrupt bank!'

Arnie walked off roaring with laughter.

11

Cliff sat and stared at his telephone. Did Arnie know something that he didn't? Was Wisconsin Credit a stupid idea after all? Was this the idea that would make him and Louise Patterson a lot of money – or would it be the end of his career?

12

Should Cliff try to sell Louise the Wisconsin Credit bonds?

Free discussion

Word file

a killing	a lot of money earned in a short time
hot tip	a valuable piece of information

Decisionmaker
Wall Street Blues

© Cambridge University Press 1997

Analysis

The characters

Read the three speeches and answer these questions:

Responsibilities...

1 Who tries to build long term relationships with customers?
2 Who looks after money for other people?
3 Who looks for and sells bonds that will increase in value?

...and attitudes

4 Who doesn't like making mistakes?
5 Who likes to do the unexpected?
6 Who has a negative attitude to younger people?

What opinions have you formed of the three characters? Discuss these questions:

1 Whose advice would you trust?
2 Which character do you think will make most money in his/her career?

The situation

Read the situation and discuss your answers to these questions:

1 What would you do if Cliff had sold you the $77 million of bonds in the
  New York property company?
   a) Sell the bonds immediately in case they continue to fall in value.
   b) Keep the bonds and hope that their price goes up.
   c) Forget about the bonds and concentrate on your next deal.
2 If you were Louise Patterson, how would you feel at the end of the
  phone call from Cliff?
   a) relieved
   b) suspicious
   c) optimistic
   d) angry

The idea

The newspaper says that Wisconsin Credit bank is facing bankruptcy, but
Cliff sees this as 'a golden investment opportunity'. Divide into pairs and,
in your own words, explain to each other why Cliff thinks this.

Read to the end of the story and then move on to discuss your decision.

Decisionmaker
**Wall Street
Blues**

© Cambridge
University Press
1997

The decision

Decision time

Should Cliff Addis try to sell Wisconsin Credit bonds to his best customer?

Try thinking about the problem in this way:

Three sides to the story

Discussion

Divide into three groups. Each group should look at the problem from the point of view of one of the main characters, by discussing one of these questions:

Group 1 – from Cliff's point of view: Why is it a good idea to try to sell Wisconsin Credit bonds to Louise Patterson?

Group 2 – from Arnie's point of view: Why is it a bad idea to try to sell Wisconsin Credit bonds to Louise Patterson?

Group 3 – from Louise's point of view: What would you do if Cliff Addis tried to sell you Wisconsin Credit bonds?

Role play

Divide into pairs with members of another group, and role play the following situations:

1 A planning meeting: Cliff explains to Arnie which bonds he intends to recommend to his customers and why. (For people from Groups 1 and 2.)
2 A sales pitch: Cliff phones Louise and tries to sell her the Wisconsin Credit bonds. (For people from Groups 2 and 3.)
3 A phone call: Louise phones Arnie and asks for some advice before buying the Wisconsin Credit bonds. (For people from Groups 1 and 3.)

Now decide!

So, should Cliff try to sell the bonds to Louise? If your discussions so far haven't produced a consensus, take a vote on it.

Photocopiable

Decisionmaker
**Wall Street
Blues**

© Cambridge
University Press
1997

At a glance

Topic:	Finance
New vocabulary:	Investment banking, the bond market
Scenario:	An American bond salesperson has to decide whether to recommend a highly risky investment to his best customer.

Answers

Way in

Most people find that when they are winning they take the money (this is the smaller risk, because there's no chance of getting nothing), but when they are losing they take the 85% chance (this is the bigger risk, because they could lose even more money). Could this explain why markets rise slowly and fall suddenly?

Analysis

The characters

1 Arnie	2 Louise	3 Cliff
4 Louise	5 Cliff	6 Arnie

The situation

You decide!

The idea

This activity gives you an opportunity to check that the learners have got the situation clear in their own minds.

Summary

The decisionmaker	Cliff Addis
The decision	Should Cliff Addis try to sell Wisconsin Credit bonds to his best customer?
The issues	1 Cliff has already recommended a bad investment to Louise. Should he risk recommending another one?
	2 It's Cliff's job to assess the risks of investments and to make recommendations to his customers. Should he trust his judgement?
	3 Cliff doesn't have the support of the senior salesperson Arnie Arnopp. Should he do something which his superior thinks is stupid?

Suggested activity

Follow the procedure set down in the 'Decision time' section (discussion → role play → vote). It's probably best if the students do both the role plays for which they're prepared before coming to a decision.

If you have fewer than six people in the class, ask each person to prepare a point of view by him/herself and then do whichever role plays are possible with the combinations of points of view that have been prepared.

A possible solution

Cliff Addis should trust his own judgement. If he thinks that Wisconsin Credit is a good opportunity for his customer, then he should recommend it without hesitation. Everybody in the financial markets knows that prices move up as well as down – and investors and salespeople have to accept that they will sometimes make mistakes. It's just part of the job!

Dirty Work

Before you read

If you want to find out more about business and the environment, read this background box:

Background

> **Business and the environment**
>
> Over the past few years, businesses have become increasingly concerned about their impact on the environment. In part, this is a response to customers who are demanding more environmentally-friendly products, but tough new environmental laws have also changed business attitudes. In some countries, politicians would like to introduce a law that would make manufacturers responsible not only for making the product but also for disposing of it at the end of its useful life.

Way in

Most people would agree that protecting the environment is a good thing. But are we prepared to pay the price? Discuss these situations:

1 You are president of a small, poor country which has only one modern hospital. Your power stations are old and produce a lot of pollution. You have received a grant of several million dollars: what do you do – build a hospital or improve your power stations?

2 Choose between these alternatives:
   a) An extremely safe modern plant that processes nuclear waste will be built near to your home or
   b) The same nuclear waste will be exported to a poor country and processed in an old-fashioned plant with few safety checks or regulations.

Decisionmaker
Dirty Work

© Cambridge University Press 1997

Dirty Work

Problem

As Carmen de Souza drove into downtown São Paulo, she could hear her baby son, Wagner, coughing in the back seat. She wished that she didn't have to bring him into the dirty, polluted city every day, but in her situation, she had no choice. As a single mother, Carmen desperately needed the money she earned working as a Sales Administrator for Archanjo, a big Brazilian cosmetics company – and that meant that on weekdays she had to leave Wagner in the care of her mother, who lived close to her office. She dropped Wagner off just before eight and was at her desk a few minutes later. She sighed as she saw yet another official letter from Archanjo's management at the top of her in-tray.

Archanjo
A Greener Future

Dear Colleague,

Last winter, a leading business journal described Archanjo as 'the dirty old man of Brazil'. According to the article, our record on toxic emissions and waste disposal was threatening not only the environment, but also our competitiveness in the international marketplace.

The new management team at Archanjo took these allegations very seriously – which is why we have come up with a new green corporate strategy, designed to limit the environmental impact of Archanjo's operations. In due course, you will receive a booklet detailing the strategy in full, but here are five of the main proposals:

1   Production will be moved away from three of our oldest and most polluting plants.

2   Our main product range will be re-packaged using exclusively bio-degradable materials.

3   A working party will look into ways of recycling waste products and using renewable energy sources in production.

4   A new computer network and e-mail system will eliminate virtually all paper from Archanjo's main offices.

5   New flexible working patterns at head office will minimise commuting by staff during the congested and polluting rush hours.

We feel sure that we can count on your support as Archanjo does its best to make Brazil and the world a better, cleaner, healthier place.

Dr Amadeus Azevedo, Chief Executive Officer

Word file

single mother	a woman raising her child or children alone
toxic emissions	poisonous waste
allegations	an accusation made without any proof
environmental impact	the effect on the environment
in due course	at the right time
to re-package	to change the container and wrapping of a product
bio-degradable	can be broken down by natural processes
to recycle	to use something again
renewable energy sources	sources like the sun or wind that are not destroyed in the process of making energy
to commute	to travel (a long distance) between home and work
e-mail	electronic mail
congested	blocked
rush hour	the times in the day when most people are travelling between home and work

Decisionmaker
Dirty Work

© Cambridge University Press 1997

Carmen didn't normally take much notice of documents from the company's management, but she was a strong supporter of the Green movement and she was pleased to see that at last Archanjo was taking its environmental responsibilities seriously. At least that's what she thought until she read the piece of paper that was handed to her that lunch time.

NO TO FACTORY CLOSURES! **NO** TO REDUNDANCIES! **NO** TO 'THE GREENER FUTURE'!

Archanjo is making the world a better, cleaner, healthier place? Don't make us laugh.
Archanjo doesn't care about the environment any more than it cares about its employees. Here's what their so-called 'greener future' really means:

They say...	But what that really means is...
Production will be moved away from three of our most polluting plants	3000 redundancies, 3000 shattered lives. We say: NO WAY!
A working party will look into recycling waste and using renewable energy	We will pay our rich friends millions of reais for yet another useless report
A new computer network and e-mail system	More redundancies, more bureaucracy
New flexible working patterns at head office will minimise commuting	Forget about your family, cancel your private life: from now on you work when we tell you

Don't be fooled. Archanjo's 'greener future' is a cynical plan to cut jobs, close factories and boost profits.

If you really care about this company's future you have no choice:

JOIN THE STRIKE AGAINST THE GREENER FUTURE FROM THIS WEDNESDAY!

Carmen read over the two documents again. She didn't like the sound of the redundancies or the new working patterns. But if she went on strike she would lose pay – and, anyway, should she really be striking against Green principles that she believed in?

Free discussion

Should Carmen join the strike on Wednesday?

Word file

the Green movement	the political movement which tries to protect the environment
redundancy	the loss of a job by an employee because there is no longer a job to do
shattered	broken
bureaucracy	unnecessary and complicated administrative procedures
to boost	to increase

Decisionmaker
Dirty Work

© Cambridge University Press 1997

Analysis

Set the scene
Read the first two paragraphs and then answer these questions:
1 Why do you think that Wagner is coughing?
2 Why does Carmen desperately need money?
3 What's her job?
4 What does Wagner do while his mother is at work?

Archanjo's letter
Read the first paragraph of the letter and then discuss this point:
1 Why might Archanjo's environmental record threaten its position in the international market?

Look at Archanjo's five proposals and then discuss these points:
2 These are four common 'Green' objectives. Discuss ways in which Archanjo's proposals might help to achieve any or all of them:
   • Reduction of air pollution
   • Saving forests
   • More efficient use of energy
   • Reduction of waste
3 Do you think that Archanjo is seriously committed to its environmental strategy?

The strike document
Read the paragraph describing Carmen's reaction and then quickly read the whole of the strike document. Then look at these two points:
1 Which of these phrases is the best description of the document?
   a) an official company document
   b) a legal document
   c) an unofficial hand out
   d) an official trade union announcement
2 Choose two adjectives that describe the tone of the document:

   sober   witty   reasoned   pompous
   sarcastic   whimsical   angry   soothing

Now, read the document more closely and discuss:
3 Which of the proposals should Carmen be worried about?
4 Which of the document's criticisms of the proposals are the <u>least</u> convincing?

Read to the end of the story and then move on to discuss your decision.

Decisionmaker
Dirty Work

© Cambridge
University Press
1997

The decision

Decision time

Should Carmen join the strike on Wednesday?

Implications 'spiders'

These two 'spiders' provide a way of organising your thoughts about the implications of Carmen's two possible decisions (to strike or not to strike). In small groups, look at the list and decide which questions are raised by which decision; then write each question next to a leg of the appropriate spider. (One question has already been written for you.)

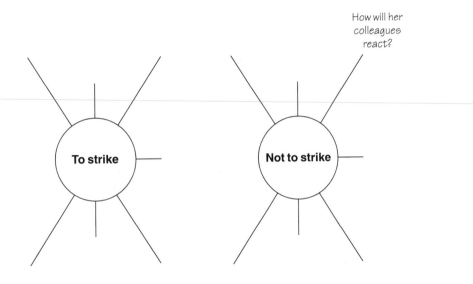

- How will her colleagues react? ✔
- What about the threat of new working patterns?
- What about her Green principles?
- How will her bosses react?
- What about money?
- What about the threat of redundancies?

If you can think of any other important implications of either decision, draw extra legs on the spiders and write questions next to them.

Now decide!

When, you've talked through all the implications of the two possible decisions, make your own choice: what should Carmen do?

Decisionmaker
Dirty Work

© Cambridge
University Press
1997

At a glance

Topic:	Business and the environment
New vocabulary:	Environmental issues
Scenario:	A Brazilian office worker has to decide whether to strike or not.

Answers

Analysis

Set the scene

1 Because of the pollution in the city.
2 Because she's a single mother.
3 She's a Sales Administrator for Archanjo.
4 He goes to his grandmother.

Archanjo's letter

1 (*suggested answer*) Because Archanjo might not conform to international environmental stándards and bad publicity might deter customers.
2 (*suggested answers*) Reduction of air pollution: proposals 1 and 5; Saving forests: proposal 3 (because it will save paper); More efficient use of energy: proposals 1 (because older plants are normally more inefficient), 3 and 5 (because cars use fuel more inefficiently in traffic jams); Reduction of waste: proposals 2, 3 and 4 (because less waste paper will be created); 3 You decide.

The strike document

1 c)
2 The tone is sarcastic and angry.
3 She should be worried about the new computer network because it could make Sales Administrators redundant, and the new working patterns because of their possible effect on her private/family life.
4 You decide.

Decision time

Implications 'spiders'

Summary

The decisionmaker	Carmen de Souza
The decision	Should she go on strike against Archanjo's proposals?
The issues	1 Are Archanjo's Green proposals a good idea? Is the company sincere in its commitment to them?
	2 What effects will the proposals have on the working lives of Carmen and her colleagues?
	3 Is a strike an appropriate or an effective response to the proposals?

A possible solution

The strike document is reasonably convincing in the way in which it casts doubt on the purity of Archanjo's motives in introducing its environmental policy. So, Carmen should feel happy that by striking she is not betraying her principles. She would also be helping to let the management know that they cannot make people redundant or change their working patterns without proper consultation.

However, striking is probably not in her own short-term personal interests, as she will lose money and may damage her relationship with her bosses. Ultimately, it is a matter for her own conscience.

Follow-up activity

Re-write the strike document, making the same points in a formal letter to Archanjo's management.

The Write Stuff

Before you read

In 'The Write Stuff', you'll read about graphology. If you'd like to know more about it read this background box:

Background

Graphology

Graphology is a way of assessing someone's character by studying his or her handwriting. In many West European countries, it is very often used by companies when they are recruiting new staff. In Switzerland, for example, graphology is used in the selection of around 75% of management jobs, and by nearly all Swiss banks. However, business-people cannot agree on whether graphology is really effective and in some countries its use is far less common. In the USA, only 5% of companies use graphology, and in the UK the figure is even lower.

You'll also read about recruitment. To think about different methods of recruitment, look at the 'Way in' section.

Way in

Using graphology is just one of many ways of choosing staff. Other methods include:

- interview
- personal recommendation
- IQ (intelligence quotient) tests
- analysis of CV
- medical tests

Can you think of any others?

Are some of these methods particularly suitable for certain jobs? Discuss which method(s) would be best when recruiting in the following cases:

- a university lecturer
- a gardener
- an army officer

Photocopial

Decisionmaker
The Write St

© Cambridge
University Pres
1997

The Write Stuff

Problem

Ingrid Wild, the personnel officer at Bayerische Bank's Frankfurt office, was outraged when she learnt that the new bank policy was to use a professional graphologist to screen all future job applicants. 'It's crazy!' she said. 'I'm the personnel professional. Everyone says I'm good at my job. I know the banking business and I understand banking people. Nobody has ever proved that graphology works – it's unscientific, irrational nonsense.'

When the post of Deputy Branch Manager in Frankfurt became vacant, Wild knew immediately who was the best person for the job – her old colleague, Siggy Altmann. They had worked together for several years at the bank's Munich head office, where Altmann had proved himself to be a quiet, methodical and efficient worker. Wild knew that Altmann was looking for promotion and when she saw his application, her mind was made up.

But, as always, her bosses insisted that she follow the correct recruitment procedure – this time including the use of a graphologist. So, working from C.V.s, as normal, Wild selected the top five candidates and then phoned to ask each of them for a handwriting sample.

'Sorry about all the fuss,' she said to Altmann on the phone. 'This graphology business is a waste of everyone's time – but it's new bank policy.'

'So, why don't you prove that it's nonsense?' Altmann said. 'It's easy to do.'

'Really?' asked Wild. 'How?'

'Just send in a copy of your own handwriting, along with all the other samples,' said Altmann, 'and then show your bosses the sort of rubbish they write about you.'

'That's a great idea, Siggy,' said Wild. 'Thank you.'

The next day, Wild sent six anonymous handwriting samples to the Frankfurt Graphology Institute – five from the job applicants and one written by herself. She labelled her own 'Sample A' and Siggy Altmann's 'Sample F'.

Wild's bosses were keen to see the results of the graphology tests and so organised a meeting with her on the day that the report was due. That morning, Wild looked through the following report with some confusion:

Decisionmaker
The Write Stuff

© Cambridge
University Press
1997

FRANKFURT GRAPHOLOGY INSTITUTE: CONFIDENTIAL REPORT

Bayerische Bank: Sample A

The handwriting is indicative of a person with considerable ambition and drive. This candidate is loyal to friends and colleagues and would make a good team member. However, s/he holds such strong views that there is almost certainly a powerful tendency to resist change at all costs. As a decisionmaker, the candidate is impulsive rather than considered in her/his judgement.

The candidate is probably not senior management material and lacks the creativity and sensitivity for such areas as trouble-shooting or human resource management. However, quick thinking and strong personality would make the candidate ideal for work as a dealer or market analyst.

FRANKFURT GRAPHOLOGY INSTITUTE: CONFIDENTIAL REPORT

Bayerische Bank: Sample F

An unusual sample, in that the candidate's writing clearly shows a recent trauma. The candidate is quiet and methodical, but certain irregularities in the script indicate unreliability when placed under any pressure.

Although the candidate has an ability to get on with other people, a low sense of self-esteem make him/her unsuitable for any position demanding leadership qualities. Nevertheless, the candidate obviously has a certain ambition and may well be able to inspire confidence in others. Probably best suited to an advisory role with limited responsibility, such as liaison or customer service officer.

Free discussion

What should Ingrid do with the reports?

Word file

personnel officer	the person responsible for matters relating to staff, such as recruitment
outraged	very angry
graphology	a way of assessing someone's character by their handwriting
to screen	to select
irrational	without reason
C.V. (curriculum vitae) BrE; AmE: résumé	a summary of a person's education, qualifications and past work experience
impulsive	thoughtless
considered	thoughtful
trouble-shooting	identifying problems in a business and putting them right
human resources management	general term for all aspects of management which deal with people
trauma	bad experience
script	handwriting
to inspire	to create
liaison officer	a person who organises the exchange of information between different departments in an organisation
customer service officer	a person who deals with the everyday demands and problems of the general public in relation to their company

Decisionmaker
The Write Stuf

© Cambridge
University Press
1997

Analysis

Read through the problem, stop at the end of each paragraph and try to answer the following questions. As you do so, discuss your answers with your colleagues:

Paragraph 1: Ingrid's responsibilities

1 Which of these alternatives best describes one of Ingrid's main responsibilities in her job?
   a) looking after the bank's day-to-day spending
   b) entertaining the bank's most important customers
   c) finding and choosing new employees
   d) writing budget forecasts
2 Why is Ingrid against graphology?

Paragraph 2: Siggy Altmann

Why does Ingrid think that Siggy Altmann is the best person for the Deputy Manager's job?

Paragraph 3: Procedures

What procedure does Ingrid have to follow when she chooses candidates for the job?

Paragraph 4: Nonsense?

1 According to Siggy, how can Ingrid show her bosses that graphology is nonsense?
2 Look at this list of adjectives and choose three which you think best describe Siggy and three which best describe Ingrid:

ambitious	efficient	innocent
loyal	confident	impulsive
practical	noisy	quiet
determined	deceitful	unprofessional

The report

In your view, are the reports reasonable assessments of Ingrid's and Siggy's characters? Compare them to your answers to the paragraph 4 question.

Now move on to discuss your decision.

Decisionmaker
The Write Stuff

© Cambridge
University Press
1997

The decision

Decision time

What should Ingrid do with the reports?

The risks

First, think about the risks she faces by completing these two sentences, using two of the phrases underneath:

If the graphologist is right about Ingrid, ...

If Ingrid's bosses accept the report on Siggy, ...

    he won't get the job.   she won't be a personnel officer.

    she shouldn't be a personnel officer.   he wouldn't get the job.

The options

There are several options that Ingrid could take in this situation. Look at this list, and, in pairs or small groups, think of one advantage and one disadvantage for each option:

	advantage	disadvantage
Option A: Tell the bosses that the reports show that graphology is total nonsense. Use Sample A (Ingrid's one) as the example which proves the point.		
Option B: Show the bosses Samples B to F, but refuse to show them Sample A.		
Option C: Tell the bosses that the experiment with graphology was a total failure and refuse to show them any of the reports.		
Option D: Don't worry about it. Show the bosses all the reports and let them decide what to do.		

Can you think of any other options open to Ingrid?

Now decide!

What should Ingrid do?

Decisionmaker
The Write Stu

© Cambridge
University Press
1997

At a glance

Topic:	Recruitment and graphology
New vocabulary:	Recruitment, describing personality
Scenario:	A German bank introduces graphology as part of its recruitment procedures, against the wishes of its personnel officer.

Answers

Way in (*suggested answers*)

Gardener: interview, personal recommendation
University lecturer: interview, analysis of CV
Army officer: interview, medical and IQ tests

Analysis

Paragraph 1: Ingrid's responsibilities

1 (c)
2 Because she thinks it's unscientific irrational nonsense

Paragraph 2: Siggy Altmann

For three reasons: Ingrid has known Siggy for many years; Siggy is a quiet, methodical and efficient worker; Siggy is looking for promotion.

Paragraph 3: Procedures

She looks through the applicants' C.V.s, selects the five top candidates and phones them to ask for handwriting samples.

Paragraph 4: Nonsense?

1 By sending the graphologist a sample of her own handwriting and then showing her bosses what the report says about her.
2 It's up to you!

Decision time

The risks

If the graphologist is right about Ingrid, she shouldn't be a personnel officer.

If Ingrid's bosses accept the report on Siggy, he won't get the job.

Summary

The decisionmaker	Ingrid Wild
The decision	What should she do with the reports?
The risk	If Ingrid's bosses accept the graphologist's judgements, things look bad for both Ingrid and Siggy. Siggy will miss out on his promotion, and Ingrid's credibility as a personnel officer will be severely compromised.
The issues	1 How can Ingrid preserve her bosses' good opinion of her?
	2 Can she still help Siggy to get the job he wants?
	3 Should she still try to convince her bosses that graphology is 'nonsense'?

A possible solution

Ingrid Wild obviously believes strongly in her own judgement and there is no good reason for her to panic now. However, she must be able to see some elements of truth in the graphologist's report and as a rational, objective professional, she should acknowledge this.

She should allow her bosses to see the FGI's full report on the handwriting samples and should point out which of the graphologist's comments she agrees with. She should then provide her bosses with her own assessments of the candidates, based on as wide a range of sources as possible (including, of course, the graphologist's report).

In this way, Ingrid will come across as an open-minded person, not a person 'to resist change at all costs' as the graphologist described her. She won't be able to prove that graphology is 'nonsense', but she should be able to put it into perspective. Graphology, she should argue, is simply one of many tools available to the personnel professional. She, as the expert, should be free to choose which tools she uses.

Follow-up activity

Here's a chance to see how effective graphology is in analysing the handwriting of people in your class. This is a simple model of one way in which a graphologist analyses handwriting:

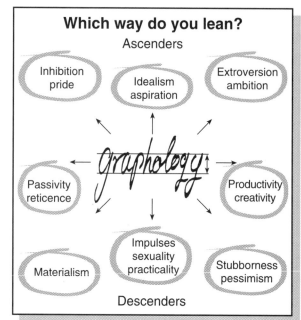

Ask everyone in the class to write the word 'graphology' on a piece of unlined paper. They should then draw a straight line roughly along the top of the g, r, a, p, o, o, g and y and another straight line under the r, a, h, o, l and o. The parts of the handwriting above the top line are called 'ascenders'; the parts below are called 'descenders'. You can assess someone's character by looking at the way in which these ascenders and descenders slope and comparing it to the chart.

Do the learners in your class agree with the results of the analysis?

Selling Your Soul

Before you read

This story is set in the music industry. If you want some background information on the pop music business, read this box:

Background

> ### The music business
>
> The pop music industry is famous for the tough contracts that it negotiates with young musicians. After a court case against his record company in 1994, the superstar George Michael described his career as 'professional slavery', because he was still subject to the conditions that he had negotiated as a young man over ten years before.
>
> Businesspeople in the music industry say that contracts need to be tough because it is such a high risk business. However, there are many stories of musicians being very badly treated, or even cheated. In 1974, the soul singer George McCrae gave away the rights to his song *Rock Your Baby* in return for the keys to a car. It was a bad mistake: the song became a huge hit and the car had been hired!

In this story, you'll read about contracts. To think about contracts in a general way, try this 'Way in' activity:

Way in

'Every time two people sign a contract, one person is making a mistake.'

Discuss these three points:

1 In your experience, is this statement true?
2 Should contracts always be fair to both sides?
3 Once a contract has been signed should people be allowed to change it?

Decisionmaker
Selling Your Soul

© Cambridge University Press 1997

Selling Your Soul

Problem

Man Egg and Johnny Bee were one of northern Europe's hottest dance acts. Music critics in the UK and Germany raved about their brilliant, original songs, and audiences loved their dynamic stage show. For the past two years, they had been playing gigs at venues across the continent three or four nights a week. But despite their hard work, Man and Johnny felt they were getting nowhere.

They believed that they were ready for a recording deal with a major label, but their manager, Bob Scolla, had other ideas. Bob had a stable of seven different acts and liked to focus his energy on one of them at a time. At the moment, he was negotiating a deal for a teenage female singer and until that deal was concluded, he refused to discuss Man and Johnny's future.

The two guys were in no position to argue. Bob Scolla had bought Man and Johnny their equipment and stage clothes, he took care of all their travelling expenses and even paid them a small weekly wage. In return, they had signed a contract that gave Bob total control over their careers: he decided which record companies they talked to, he owned 75% of the rights to their songs and even controlled their public image.

As Bob's negotiations over the teenage singer dragged on for month after month, Man and Johnny became increasingly frustrated. Then, one night, after a gig in Rotterdam, they were approached by an American music publisher.

'Hey,' she said, 'you guys have written some brilliant songs. I can't offer you a recording contract, but how about a publishing deal?' Although it wasn't exactly what they had hoped for, Man and Johnny agreed it was the best offer they had received in the past two years.

Word file

hottest	most exciting
an act	a performer or group of performers
music critics	journalists who write reports about records and concerts
to rave about	to be very positive and enthusiastic about
brilliant	(here) excellent
gig	a concert or job (music industry slang)
venue	a place where concerts are staged
recording deal	a contract with a music company to perform and record music
major label	a big record company
stable	a number of performers managed by the same person
rights to	ownership of
to drag on	to continue for a long time
music publisher	a company or person that prints and distributes music and lyrics
guys	men
publishing deal	a contract to print and distribute music and lyrics

The next day, they met with Bob Scolla and asked to be released from their contract, to sign the deal with the American publisher. Bob smiled. 'Sure', he said, 'You can do that – but, if you do, I will never do anything to help you again. Understand? Oh, and there's one more thing –'

'What's that?' asked Johnny.

'I keep my 75% rights to your first forty songs,' Bob said. 'After all, I've paid for them.'

'But… but…' Johnny stammered, 'we've only written thirty.'

Free discussion

Should Man and Johnny stay with Bob? Should they leave him and sign a publishing deal? Is there a third way?

Analysis

Paragraphs 1 to 3: Getting nowhere?

Read the first three paragraphs and then summarise the situation by answering these four questions:

1   What is Man and Johnny's main objective?
2   Why does Bob Scolla refuse to discuss Man and Johnny's future?
3   What does Bob do for Man and Johnny?
4   What does he get in return?

Does Man and Johnny's arrangement with Bob Scolla seem to be fair to both sides?

Paragraph 4: A gig in Rotterdam

Read the fourth paragraph and then decide which of these sentences are true and which are false:

1   Bob's negotiations over the teenage singer continued for a long time.
2   Man and Johnny arranged a meeting with a Dutch music publisher.
3   The music publisher offered Man and Johnny a recording deal.
4   Man and Johnny felt that the music publisher's deal was unfair.

Paragraph 5: We've only written thirty!

Read the final paragraph and then discuss these two points:

1   Do you think that Bob Scolla's condition is reasonable?
2   What would you do if you were in his position?

Now, think about the situation from Man and Johnny's point of view, by doing the 'Decision time' activity.

Decisionmaker
Selling Your Soul

© Cambridge University Press 1997

The decision

Decision time

Should Man and Johnny stay with Bob?
Should they leave him and sign a publishing deal? Is there a third way?

Pros and cons

Discuss the first two alternatives that Man and Johnny have, and draw up a list of pros and cons for each.

Stay with Bob		Publishing deal	
Pros	Cons	Pros	Cons

Do either of the alternatives discussed above sound like the best solution to Man and Johnny's problem? If so – take your decision!

If not, try this technique to help you to think more creatively about their situation:

Analogy

When there is no obvious solution to a problem, businesspeople can help themselves to think creatively by comparing the problem to a different but similar situation – an analogy. Here is an example of an analogy to Man and Johnny's situation:

> There is a rare animal in your local zoo. Lots of people would like to see this rare animal, but for some reason, the zoo authorities will not show it to the public. How would you persuade the authorities to allow people to see this animal?

Briefly, discuss possible solutions to the analogy. Then, discuss the three questions:

1 What similarities are there between the analogy and Man and Johnny's situation?
2 Do the solutions to the analogy suggest any solutions to Man and Johnny's problem?
3 Can you think of any other analogies to Man and Johnny's problem?

Now decide!

What should Man and Johnny do?

Decisionmaker
Selling Your Soul

© Cambridge University Press 1997

At a glance

Topic:	Contracts in the pop music industry
New vocabulary:	Music industry
Scenario:	Two young musicians are trapped by a contract which threatens their careers.

Answers

Analysis

Paragraphs 1 to 3: Getting nowhere?

1 They want to get a recording deal with a major label.

2 Because he's focussing his energies on another act.

3 He buys them clothes, equipment and pays travelling expenses and a small wage.

4 Total control over their careers: he decides which record companies they talk to, he owns 75% of the rights to all their songs and he controls their public image.

Paragraph 4: A gig in Rotterdam

1 true   2 false   3 false   4 false

Decision time

Pros and Cons (*suggested answers*)

Stay with Bob

Pros: 1 Bob will still look after their interests. 2 They will still have 25% of the rights to their first 40 songs.

Cons: 1 There is no guarantee that he will work harder for them in future. 2 They will always be subject to the terms of an unfavourable contract.

Publishing deal

Pros: It's the best offer they've had in the past two years.

Cons: 1 They still only get 25% of the rights to their first 40 songs – 10 of which they have not yet written! 2 They won't have a manager to look after their interests.

Summary

The decisionmakers	Man Egg and Johnny Bee
The decision	Should Man and Johnny stay with Bob? Should they leave him and sign a publishing deal? Is there a third way?

A possible solution

Man and Johnny have to find a third way. Their current management arrangement with Bob Scolla is clearly unsatisfactory, but there is no point in accepting the alternative publishing contract if their first forty songs remain his property.

This means that, for now, they will have to stay under Scolla's management. However, there is a great deal that they can do to force him to take their interests more seriously. As they are admired by both the public and the press, Man and

Johnny should try to generate as much extra publicity as they can, by offering interviews to journalists, making public appearances and 'networking' as much as possible.

If a wave of good publicity doesn't change Scolla's policy towards them, there is nothing to stop Man and Johnny contacting record companies directly themselves. Scolla probably wouldn't like it, but if Man and Johnny were successful, he's unlikely to refuse the chance of making some easy money!

Advertising Albion

Before you read

'Advertising Albion' looks at the creative side of the advertising industry. To find out more about an agency's creative department, read this background box:

Background

> **The creative department**
>
> The creative department of an advertising agency comes up with the ideas, the words and the images for adverts. It is normally divided into teams of two people – a copywriter, who writes the words, and an art director, who is responsible for the pictures and look of the advert. Creative departments can be very unconventional places: in some agencies members of the department can spend part of their day playing pool or listening to music, as they try to dream up their next campaign. But that shouldn't hide the fact that advertising is a highly pressurised and competitive industry.

To think about the effectiveness of advertising, try this 'Way in' activity:

Way in

Businesses spend roughly 3% of their revenues on advertising. As a result, some advertising agencies make millions for writing just a few words. But do companies and consumers get value for money from advertising? Discuss these questions:

1 Have you bought anything because of an advert in the past month?

2 Have you decided <u>not</u> to buy something because of an advert in the past month?

3 How many adverts currently on TV or at the cinema can you describe in detail?

4 If you had a company, which would you spend more money on – research and development or advertising?

Decisionmaker
Advertising Albion

© Cambridge University Press 1997

Advertising Albion

Problem

Jane Long was under pressure. The Bryant Long advertising agency was desperate to win the prestigious contract with Albion Airlines – but there was fierce competition from several other top agencies. As Bryant Long's creative director, Jane knew that her creative department had to come up with some brilliant ideas very, very quickly.

She decided to give her creative teams just 24 hours to deliver rough versions of their initial ideas. To help them focus on Albion's requirements, she gave all of them this summary of the advertising brief:

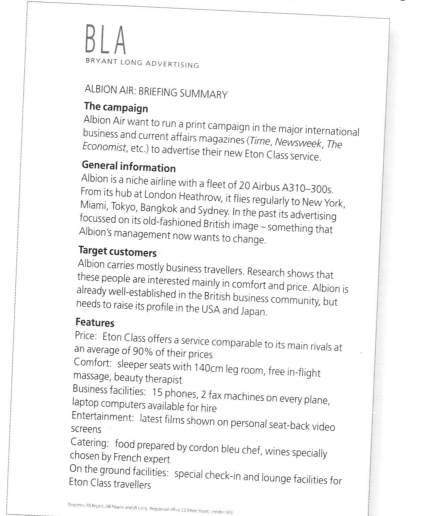

BLA
BRYANT LONG ADVERTISING

ALBION AIR: BRIEFING SUMMARY

The campaign
Albion Air want to run a print campaign in the major international business and current affairs magazines (*Time, Newsweek, The Economist*, etc.) to advertise their new Eton Class service.

General information
Albion is a niche airline with a fleet of 20 Airbus A310–300s. From its hub at London Heathrow, it flies regularly to New York, Miami, Tokyo, Bangkok and Sydney. In the past its advertising focussed on its old-fashioned British image – something that Albion's management now wants to change.

Target customers
Albion carries mostly business travellers. Research shows that these people are interested mainly in comfort and price. Albion is already well-established in the British business community, but needs to raise its profile in the USA and Japan.

Features
Price: Eton Class offers a service comparable to its main rivals at an average of 90% of their prices
Comfort: sleeper seats with 140cm leg room, free in-flight massage, beauty therapist
Business facilities: 15 phones, 2 fax machines on every plane, laptop computers available for hire
Entertainment: latest films shown on personal seat-back video screens
Catering: food prepared by cordon bleu chef, wines specially chosen by French expert
On the ground facilities: special check-in and lounge facilities for Eton Class travellers

Directors: RS Bryant, AB Mason and JS Long. Registered office 23 More Street, London W8

Word file

prestigious	important and highly respected
brief	information, instructions
print campaign	a series of adverts in magazines or newspapers
niche airline	a small airline catering for a particular type of customer
hub	the central point from which all flights leave
to raise its profile	to increase public awareness
sleeper seats	large, comfortable, reclining seats
beauty therapist/ beautician	a person who specialises in making skin, hair, etc. more beautiful
leg room	space between one plane seat and the seat in front of it
laptop computer	small portable computer
seat-back video screen	TV screens built into the back of the plane seats in front of the passengers
cordon bleu chef	an extremely good cook
on the ground facilities	the service the airline provides at airports

Decisionmaker **Advertising Albion**

© Cambridge University Press 1997

The creative teams worked all night on the brief and they all looked exhausted as they left their ideas on Jane's desk the next day. Jane looked through them anxiously.

HOW TO IMPRESS YOUR FINANCE DIRECTOR

Expenses Claim

Albion Air Eton Class
New York – London

Finance directors don't smile a lot. Trying to keep costs down without sacrificing quality is one of the toughest jobs in any company. But when your finance director sees Albion Eton Class on your next expenses claim, you can be sure that you're bringing a little happiness into his life.

That's because he knows that the price of an Albion Eton Class ticket undercuts its rivals by an average of 10%. And you know that you can always rely on Albion's unparalleled standards of comfort and service.

So keep everyone happy. Fly Albion Eton Class.

Albion Airways

Decisionmaker
**Advertising
Albion**

© Cambridge
University Press
1997

MEET THE CABIN CREW

The Comte de Saint-Loup, pictured at his fourteenth century chateau in Anjou.

He doesn't know where the lifejackets are kept. If you snapped your fingers at him, he'd almost certainly ignore you. But the Comte de Saint-Loup is a key member of the Albion Air cabin crew.

The Comte is one of France's most respected wine experts. And he uses his knowledge to help us choose the finest – and some of the rarest – wines for our Eton Class passengers. You won't always find the Comte in the cabin, but you can still sample his cellar in the air!

Albion Airways

The Comte's selection.
One of the ways in which Albion Air helps you to fly in style.

As Jane was looking at the final idea, the marketing manager of Albion rang.

'Jane,' he said, 'we need to see your best idea by 9 o'clock tomorrow morning. Can you do that?'

'No problem,' she said. 'I'll be ready with something really special.' She put down the phone and looked at the three adverts again.

Free discussion

Which advert should Jane Long choose?

Word file

masseur	a person trained to give massage
expenses claim	an office form showing how money was spent on a business trip
to sacrifice	to give up
to undercut	to offer at a lower price
unparalleled	without an equal
cabin crew	the people who look after passengers during a flight
Comte	a French aristocrat
cellar	an underground room often used for storing wine

Decisionmaker
Advertising Albion

© Cambridge University Press 1997

Analysis

The briefing summary

Read the first two paragraphs of the problem carefully. Then look at Jane Long's briefing summary and try this activity:

You are an international business traveller. Scan Jane Long's summary and choose the three most attractive things about Albion Air.

The adverts

When you've thought about Jane Long's summary and read the next paragraph, look carefully at the three advertisements and analyse them in this way:

These five techniques are often used in adverts for products and services.

- Testimonial – a customer explains why s/he particularly likes the product or service
- Focus on the 'Unique Selling Point' (USP) – the advert talks about just one aspect of the product/service
- Endorsement – someone else's glamour, charm or success is used to sell the product/service
- Promise a benefit – the advert explains how the service/product will improve the customer's life
- Story appeal – the advert tells a story in which the product/service solves a problem

Decide which of these techniques are being used in the three Albion adverts.

Advert	Technique
Meet the cabin crew	....
How to impress the Finance Director	....
Spot the difference	....

Now move on to make your decision.

Decisionmaker
Advertising Albion

© Cambridge University Press 1997

The decision

Decision time

Which advert should Jane Long choose to present to the Albion management?

Assessment

Here's a way of assessing the three adverts that the creative teams have produced:
Advertising people often assess the effectiveness of adverts by these criteria:

- **Image** What image does the advert convey?
- **Positioning** What does the product do and who is it for?
- **Unique Selling Point (USP)** What makes the product different from its competitors?
- **Benefits** In what ways can this product help the customer?

Assess the three adverts by these criteria, using the questions to help you. Give a score from 1 (lowest) to 10 (highest) for how well you think each advert succeeds in each of the categories.

	Marks		
	Spot the difference	How to impress…	Meet the…
Image Does the advert have the right image for the target customers? Does it have the right image for the airline?			
Positioning Does the advert give a good idea of the service the airline offers? Does it explain who the service is for?			
Unique selling point (USP) Does the advert make Albion seem different from other airlines?			
Benefits Does the advert explain how Albion will help its customers?			

Now add up the scores: which advert has the highest score?

Before you take your decision, think about the following:
Do you think that the advert with the highest score is really the best one?
Should Jane ask the creative teams to come up with some more ideas?

Now decide!

What should Jane do?

Decisionmaker
**Advertising
Albion**

© Cambridge
University Press
1997

At a glance

Topic:	Advertising
New vocabulary:	Advertising, air travel
Scenario:	An advertising agency is asked to come up with ideas for a campaign to advertise a small but prestigious airline.

Answers

Analysis

The adverts

These adverts, like most others, make use of several different techniques at the same time. However, these are the suggested answers:

Meet the cabin crew: Unique Selling Point/Endorsement

How to impress the finance director: Promise a Benefit

Spot the difference: Testimonial/Endorsement

Summary

The decisionmaker	Jane Long
The decision	Which advert should she choose to show to the Albion management?
The issues	1 Which advert is the best?
	2 Will Jane get any better results if she asks her creative people for more ideas? (Remember, they've all been up all night already.)

Suggested activity: Client presentation

Divide the class into groups or pairs, and ask them to work on a different advert. Each group or pair should prepare a presentation of its advert to the management of Albion Air. The presentation should include:

1 Introduction
2 Albion's requirements
3 Image and positioning
4 USP and benefits
5 Creative aspects and techniques of the advert
6 Conclusion

A possible solution

There's no point in asking the exhausted creative teams to come up with any more ideas, so Jane must choose one of the three adverts that are in front her. All three of

them respond intelligently to the brief and a strong case can be made for each one.

'Meet The Cabin Crew' is strong on image and USP, but is weaker on positioning and only really promises benefits to wine drinkers. 'How To Impress Your Finance Director...' promises a strong benefit and positions Albion clearly, but perhaps undermines the airline's image by focussing on its low price. 'Spot The Difference' is possibly the most effective: it gives the airline an attractive image, positions it correctly and promises that travellers will arrive feeling refreshed and ready to do business.

Follow-up activity

Ask the students to create their own adverts for Albion Air.

Hard Times

Before you read

In 'Hard Times' you'll read about the world of telesales. To find out some more about it, read this background box:

Background

Telesales

Telesales people try to sell products or services to people over the telephone. It's a very efficient way of selling because they don't spend time and money on travelling. But it's not always easy to sell something that the customer can't see, so they need to be very persuasive. Success is always very important to telesales people, because their earnings often depend on how much they sell. As a result, the atmosphere in telesales offices can be extremely pressurised and competitive.

Try this 'Way in' activity to think about sales and salespeople in general:

Way in

Discuss these questions:

1 When you buy something, which of these factors has the biggest influence on your decision?
   - the product
   - the price
   - the advertising
   - the salesperson

2 Do you think it's fair to pay salespeople according to how much they sell?

Decisionmaker
Hard Times

© Cambridge
University Press
1997

Hard Times

Problem

Recession had hit the advertising telesales team at Bluebird Publications hard. No one wanted to buy advertising space in Bluebird's range of glossy up-market lifestyle magazines any more. Even the telesales team leader, Rob Grewal – the company's number one salesperson – was finding it difficult to close more than one or two deals a week. As each salesperson's income depended entirely on commission from business that he or she personally generated, competition between salespeople was fiercer than ever.

Everybody agreed it was the worst possible time for young Duncan Black to join the department – particularly since it was Duncan's first job and he seemed to lack the obvious qualities needed to succeed as a salesperson. But after only two days in the office, Duncan put down his telephone and smiled to himself. He had just closed a deal for a twelve-month order for full colour double page adverts in Bluebird's most prestigious publication. It was worth as much commission as many of the others earned in six good weeks. Rob Grewal was amazed; it was the sort of deal he dreamt about.

'Which company is it, Duncan?' he asked. 'Who's it with?'

'Paxham's Menswear,' said Duncan.

'Paxham's?' exclaimed Grewal. 'But everyone in this office has tried to get Paxham's a hundred times. Paxham's don't buy advertising space! It's against their corporate policy.'

In the pub that lunchtime, Grewal raged against young Black's good fortune. 'What does that kid know?' he shouted. 'We've all been softening up Paxham's for years. I've spent hours of my life on the phone to their marketing department. Then that kid comes along and reaps the reward for all our hard work with just one five-minute phone call. Times are hard for all of us, aren't they? I say we split his commission between everyone in the office. It's only fair.'

A few of the telesales people nodded their heads in agreement. Others looked uncomfortable. 'Come on, Rob,' said one of them. 'A year ago, when you had all the luck, no one asked you to share it with them, did they?'

Grewal looked at him coldly. 'In my case,' he said, 'it wasn't luck. I got where I am by hard work.'

Photocopiable

Decisionmaker
Hard Times

© Cambridge
University Press
1997

When they returned from lunch, Duncan Black was not yet back at his desk. So, when Black's telephone started ringing, Rob Grewal answered it. '... Sure,' said Grewal. '... Sure, you don't need to speak to Mr Black. I can take your order. I'm Mr Black's boss. Now, what would you like? ... A full colour back page? ... Certainly... If you can fax through confirmation of that, with 'Order taken by Mr Grewal' at the bottom of the letter, that would be great... Thank you, it was a pleasure doing business with you.'

As Grewal put down the telephone several of his colleagues looked at him suspiciously. 'You're not going to claim the commission on that order, are you?' asked one of them.

'Of course,' said Grewal.

'But, that was Duncan's client,' said another. 'Duncan has done all the work to get that business. It should be his commission. Come on, we're a team. We have to trust each other.'

Grewal smiled at the other telesales people. 'I don't care who did the work,' he said. 'I took the order, so I say that's my commission. He should have been back from lunch on time.'

'Now, listen, Rob,' said one of the older salespeople, 'we're all upset about that Paxham order. But that's life, isn't it? It's no reason for you to steal one of Duncan's other clients.'

Grewal glared at his colleagues. 'It's my commission,' he repeated. 'And I'm the team leader. So, what are you going to do about it?'

Free discussion

Should the other members of the telesales team allow Rob Grewal to claim the commission on the new order?

Word file

recession	a period of reduction in business activity
advertising space	an area of a magazine or newspaper for advertisements
glossy	shiny, expensive
up-market	sophisticated, expensive
lifestyle magazines	magazines about fashion, famous people, travel, homes etc.
telesales	selling of goods and services by telephone
to close a deal	to make a sale
commission	a payment made to a salesperson when s/he makes a sale
to generate	to make
obvious qualities	skills needed for a job
prestigious	important and highly respected
corporate policy	a plan, or set of ideas, of behaviour agreed by a company
kid	child (slang)
to soften up	to establish friendly relations before trying to make a sale
to reap the reward	to get the benefit
Come on	an expression used to express lack of belief

Decisionmaker
Hard Times

© Cambridge
University Press
1997

Analysis

Paragraph 1: Why are times so hard?

Read the first paragraph of the problem and then complete the flow chart:

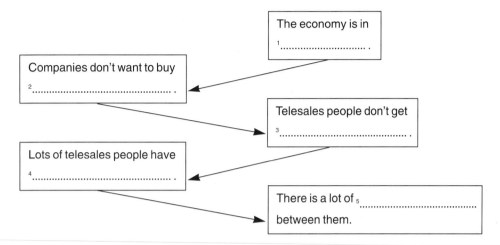

The economy is in
1............................ .

Companies don't want to buy
2.. .

Telesales people don't get
3.. .

Lots of telesales people have
4.. .

There is a lot of 5....................................
between them.

Paragraph 2: The perfect salesperson?

When you've read the second paragraph, think about what qualities you need to become a good salesperson. Number these qualities in order of importance, with 1 the most important:

☐ determination   ☐ the ability to get on with people

☐ good luck   ☐ intelligence

☐ the ability to listen   ☐ self-confidence

☐ ruthlessness   ☐ personal charm

Paragraphs 3 and 4: Why's he angry?

Read paragraphs 3 and 4 and then answer this question:

Why do you think Rob Grewal is so angry? Choose a reason from this list:

a) Because he doesn't like Duncan.

b) Because he thinks that Duncan doesn't deserve the commission on the Paxham's order.

c) Because he's tried (and failed) to get business from Paxham's many times.

d) Because he wants the money that Duncan's going to get.

Paragraphs 5 and 6: Get the facts straight

When you've read paragraphs 5 and 6, check your facts by answering these five questions:

1 Who made the sale to Paxham's?   4 Who should get the commission?

2 Who should get the commission?   5 Who's claiming the commission?

3 Who made the new sale?

Character profile: Rob Grewal

When you've read the whole story, think about the character of Rob Grewal. Choose three adjectives from this list which you think best describe him:

generous   aggressive   persuasive   mean

selfish   tough   kind   arrogant

Compare your description with the qualities of a good salesperson that you chose earlier. Do you think he deserves to be team leader?

Now move on and make your decision!

Photocopiable

Decisionmaker
Hard Times

© Cambridge
University Press
1997

The decision

Decision time

Should the telesales people allow Rob to claim the commission on the new order?

What are the options?

There are many different possible responses to this situation and many possible courses of action. To help you think through the possibilities, try this activity:
In the left-hand column, there are five different ways of responding to the situation. In the right-hand column, there are five different courses of action that the telesales people can take. Match the response on the left to the course of action on the right:

Response	**Course of action**
• confrontation	• tell Rob that you'll keep quiet about the commission if he shares it with you
• go straight to the top	• suggest that Rob and Duncan share the commission
• ignore the problem	• report Rob's action to a superior
• get something for yourself	• tell Rob that he's totally wrong and that he must return the commission
• compromise	• keep quiet

Discuss the various courses of action. Which course of action would you choose?

Now decide!

Decisionmaker
Hard Times

© Cambridge
University Press
1997

At a glance

Topic:	Telesales
New vocabulary:	Sales
Scenario:	A new member of a telesales team makes his boss very angry when he makes a lucky sale.

Answers

Way in

The four factors given here are a slight variation on the four 'P's of the marketing mix – product, price, promotion and place. Marketing theory says that all of these factors have a great influence on consumer choice.

Analysis

Paragraph 1: Why are times so hard?
1 recession
2 advertising space
3 commission
4 financial problems
5 competition

Paragraph 2: The perfect salesperson?
You decide!

Paragraphs 3 and 4: Why's he angry?
Suggested answer: (b), and possibly (c) and (d) as well!

Paragraphs 5 and 6: Get the facts straight
1–4 Duncan   5 Rob

Character profile: Rob Grewal
Suggested answers: selfish, aggressive, arrogant

Decision time

What are the options?

confrontation: tell Rob that he's totally wrong

go straight to the top: report Rob's action to a superior

ignore the problem: keep quiet

get something for yourself: tell Rob that you'll keep quiet if he shares Duncan's commission with you

compromise: suggest that Rob and Duncan share the commission

Summary

The decisionmakers	The telesales people (not Rob or Duncan)
The decision	Should they allow Rob Grewal to claim the commission on the new order?
The issues	1 Duncan is new and Rob is the team leader. Is it worth making Rob angry by arguing with him?
	2 Rob worked hard to get the Paxham's order, but in the end Duncan got the commission. Duncan did the work on the new order and now Rob is claiming the commission. What's the difference between the two cases?
	3 If Rob is allowed to claim Duncan's commission, can the members of the team ever trust each other again?

Suggested activity: Persuasion

With groups of six or less, this activity can be staged as a discussion (assuming there is disagreement!). With a larger group, follow this procedure:

Ask for a show of hands to find out who has chosen which response/course of action from the 'Decision time' section. Organise the students into groups, each one with as broad a mix of opinion as possible. Set a time limit of ten or fifteen minutes and then get each group to try to agree on a course of action. The groups should then try to come to a class decision.

A possible solution

There is a clear difference between Duncan's actions in getting the Paxham's commission and Rob's claim to the commission on the new order. The first case is just a lucky break; the second is not very different from straightforward theft.

Although the atmosphere at Bluebird is very competitive, the members of the telesales team have to be able to trust each other. They should therefore first make it clear to Rob Grewal that his claim to Duncan's commission is quite wrong and give him the chance to change his position. If he doesn't do this, the telesales team have no choice but to report Rob's conduct to a superior in the company.